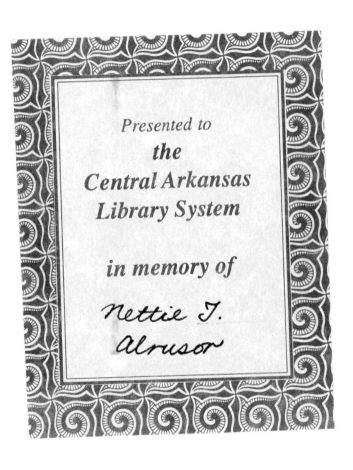

Memory Fields

SHLOMO BREZNITZ

Alfred A. Knopf
New York
1993

An excerpt from this work was published in Parade magazine.

Grateful acknowledgment is made to Plenum Publishing Corp. for permission to reprint an excerpt from chapter 15 by Shlomo Breznitz in The Dynamics of Stress: Physiological and Social Perspectives, edited by M. Appley and Richard Trumbull (Plenum Publishing Corp., 1986).

Library of Congress Cataloging-in-Publication Data
Breznitz, Shlomo.
Memory fields / by Shlomo Breznitz. — 1st ed.
p.   cm.
ISBN 0-679-40403-1
1. Breznitz, Shlomo—Childhood and youth.
2. Jews—Czechoslovakia—Persecutions.
3. Holocaust, Jewish (1939–1945—Czechoslovakia—Personal narratives.
4. World War, 1939–1945—Children—Czechoslovakia.   I. Title.
DS135.C97B74   1993
943.7′004924—dc20   92-17323   CIP

Manufactured in the United States of America

First Edition

*This book is dedicated
to my sister, Judith,
and to the memory
of our parents.*

Acknowledgments

IT TOOK A FRIEND'S active intervention to overcome my procrastination in writing these memoirs. I am grateful to Walter Anderson for engaging me in a venture that turned out to be personally enriching. It was my good fortune to work at Knopf with Ashbel Green, a vice president and senior editor turned prime counsel. I owe special thanks to Jan Urban for helping me to find Sister Koletta. It transformed the journey back into a unique experience. The gentle interest of friends provided much-needed encouragement. My wife and children, who knew how difficult it was for me to dwell on these events, made it possible.

Prologue

MY STORY IS ABOUT an earthquake—one pro-
duced by men. The most powerful ever, it had millions of
epicenters. As a child who happened to be in the wrong
place at the wrong time, caught in the maelstrom of events,
I, too, became its epicenter. Instead of seconds, this "man-
quake" took years, and its aftershocks are still troubling
our planet. Among its casualties was human innocence,
finally and irrevocably erased from the dealings of men and
nations.

For many years, the memories of these events have
toyed with me. While some loose fragments were always
available and could be summoned at will, others were
more elusive; they would surface briefly, tempting pursuit,
only to be lost the next moment. And then there was yet
another type of memory, whose existence was suggested
by the gaping holes in the story of my childhood. It seemed
buried under the rubble of its aftermath. For too long it
was inaccessible, its secrets conveniently locked behind
the faithful bars of repression.

Then, one day, the recognition of its loss became too obvious, and the absence of a coherent past disturbing and intriguing at the same time. Over the years, the efforts to retrieve this largely dark part of my early life were only partially successful, and thus the serious attempt by its rightful owner to reclaim that memory had to wait for the writing of this book.

The truth, however, is an easy prey, and its enemies are many. Chief among them are the various pretenders, whose truthlike appearance can easily fool the naive and the skeptical alike. Cloaked in shreds of well-remembered details, their own different versions of the story invariably impose some type of self-serving interpretation.

There are many different truths, all quite plausible, and often very tempting. And then there is time, which plays tricks of its own. The fields of memory are like a rich archeological site, with layer upon layer of artifacts from different periods, which, through some geological upheaval, got mixed up. Since it is the upheaval itself that is the stuff my story is made of, only part of the truth survived.

Good faith by itself is not sufficient to transform personal recollections into history, and mine, too, are at best a story.

Memory Fields

Back to Safety

Out of this nettle, danger,
we pluck this flower,
safety.

SHAKESPEARE,
Henry IV, Part One

I WAS AWAKENED in the middle of the night, but this time gently, by the soft touch of my mother's lips on my forehead.

"Quick, get up. We are leaving the camp."

"What? Are they taking us on the transport?"

"Sh . . . whisper, nobody must know that we are leaving. And no, it is not the transport. Apuka [Father] has arranged for our release."

Still half asleep, slow to comprehend what was happening, I recalled the other awakening. It was a Friday night—they always preferred the Sabbath for their unholy actions—and the loudspeaker could hardly be heard above the noise of crying and shouting. Names were called, summoning their bearers to get ready for immediate transport to Auschwitz. It was 1942, and even I, a child of six, knew what that meant. The implications of words like "Auschwitz" and "transport" spread like the plagues of earlier times across Europe.

They started by announcing the names in alphabetical order, and since ours began with a *B,* Anyuka [Mother] released the pressure of her hug almost imperceptibly once they passed our letter. But our relief was cut short when they suddenly reversed direction and started calling names in backward alphabetical order. Then, for some reason that only "they" could comprehend, the names began to be called in what appeared to be an entirely random fashion. No, there was nothing that night which one could cling to for a sense of safety, and the powerful smell of fear was nauseating even within the comfort of Anyuka's hug. They must have enjoyed their power to frighten at least as much as their power to kill.

Our names were not called, and in the early hours of the morning, in a much less crowded barrack, utterly exhausted, I went back to sleep.

Tonight it was the silence that frightened me. Are we doing something that was forbidden? So many things were forbidden that one could never be sure. Would the guards find us out and put us on the next transport? Could what Anyuka said be true? I had not seen my father for almost two months, since he had not been at home when the three of us were suddenly rounded up.

For some time now we had been living in the small village of Vrbove, about an hour's train ride from Bratislava, where he worked. Apuka had chosen this village in the hope that it was too small and too remote for "them" to bother with.

"Quick, get dressed. We must be gone," whispered my sister, Judith, who was four years older than me. She was obviously anxious to help Mother, who was trying to collect our belongings. (After that first Friday night of terror I had refused to change into my pajamas at night, insisting on sleeping with all my clothes on, ready for the journey. It was only after a few nights of undisturbed sleep that I agreed to undress, keeping my clothes under the mattress.)

The next thing I remember is one of the guards ushering us between the beds, people waking up and eyeing us uncomprehendingly, then being out in the rainy night, hit by the freshness of the air, and moving swiftly between the other barracks and, unbelievably, toward the gate. Judith squeezed my hand in anticipation, just as she would on that other fateful day several years later.

Words were exchanged in hushed voices, and we were all pushed inside a small car. Apuka was at the wheel, but not until we put some distance between us and the camp did we allow ourselves to express the happiness of our reunion. The night was damp and cold, and our breath soon covered the windows with a heavy mist, shutting everything out. Inside the small car we hugged one another, and I was absolutely convinced that nothing bad could befall me ever again.

·   ·   ·

W H A T   W A S   T H I S   T H I N G   happening all around us? We were changing places, friends, and schools, and we were always in a hurry. It looked to me as if we were running away. But from whom? The Germans? I had not yet seen a single German soldier, only the Slovak Guards, with swastikas of their own, acting as surrogates.

At school we were taught to sing the Slovak national anthem while holding our right hands high up in the air, with our arms fully extended, in the manner of the official Nazi salute. I found it difficult to keep my arm straight throughout the entire song, and one of my greatest worries was that "they" would see it was shaking. It would be terrible. They would surely ask me to remove my pants to check whether I was Jewish, for only a Jewish boy would do a thing like that.

For some time now I had known that whatever happened, I must never let anyone remove my pants or watch me while I was peeing. I could not remember who had explained this to me, perhaps Apuka, but I knew it, and I was scared every time I had to pee in a public place. Later, in the orphanage, I often delayed going to the bathroom, preferring to wet my pants rather than take the chance of exposing myself.

[I T   I S   1 9 7 7 , and I am on an official visit to West Germany. It is the first day of my first visit there, and I have just arrived at the Cologne airport. I need to use the restroom. I have been to public restrooms hundreds of times at airports all over the world, and I realize that nowadays many non-Jews are circumcised. But suddenly, after all these years, the panic resurges, and I am afraid that the person standing next to me will find me out.]

THIS "THING" AROUND ME had yet another face. There were new words, which even the adults dreaded: "Auschwitz," "transport," "Gestapo," "SS." Later, there were more of them.

People whom I loved kept disappearing, one by one. Grandma and Grandpa disappeared. Uncle Jozhko disappeared. He was a deaf-mute and used to take me strolling along the river when we visited with Grandpa and Grandma. I liked him a lot. Aunt Ilonka, Uncle Hanzi, and my cousins Palko and Andy disappeared. Anyuka often cried, and I would see her wiping her eyes and attempting to hide it. And Apuka was never there; he worked far away in Bratislava and came home only on weekends. We all used to live in Bratislava in the "good old days." Judith explained to me that he was a very important engineer and that "they" needed him, and that President Tiso himself had given Apuka a piece of paper indicating that he was special and should not be taken on the transport. It all sounded very complicated, but when I saw Apuka that night at the wheel of the car freeing us from the camp, my confidence in the future was restored.

Rivers

Midnight shakes the
memory
As a madman shakes a
dead geranium.

T. S. ELIOT,
"Rhapsody on a Windy Night"

THE CAMP WAS IN ZILINA, and when Apuka
got us out we stayed in the town. I took it as just another
of the meaningless coincidences that governed our lives
during that insane period of European history. It was only
forty-six years later, as I was flying with Elie Wiesel from
Paris to Cracow on a visit to Auschwitz, that I realized
Zilina was just across the border from Auschwitz. What
appeared to be a meaningless coincidence turned out to be
part of the well-organized murder machine. The camp was

there because it was a major railway depot, a good staging ground for transports to Auschwitz.

In the Slovak language, "zila" means vein, and "Zilina" refers to the several rivers that crisscross this mountainous region like veins. It was the rail tracks, however, rather than the rivers that, like veins, carried the blood of the victims to their final destination.

WITH ONE OF THESE rivers I associate a particularly happy time and the few sketchy memories I have of my father:

A family picnic on a beautiful summer Sunday. Apuka was barefoot, and his head was closely cropped. He suggested a race. We started off, and although I was doing quite well at first, he suddenly gained speed and won by a great margin. I was gasping for air and bursting with happiness. . . . I recall Apuka searching for flat stones on the riverbank and throwing them so that they jumped on the water one . . . two . . . three . . . four times or more. I was fascinated and frantically searched for more stones.

And Apuka showing us how to make a mirror by putting saliva on a stalk of straw. He broke the tiny stalk in two places, pulled the ends close together, and placed the broken part in his mouth. Next he slowly pushed the sides apart, stretching the saliva more and more to produce a triangular mirror. A miracle. But what a precarious mirror it was! Overstretched by just a fraction of an inch, the delicate film would burst, revealing just a broken straw and a gaping hole.

The river was well below its spring flooding level, and

there was a strong smell of baked mud. To this day such a smell brings out in me a mysterious feeling of excitement. Here is one such occasion:

I T   W A S   T H E   S U M M E R   of 1959, and there were six of us on a train from Budapest to Yugoslavia—five students representing Israel at the Student Chess Olympics and our trainer, Moshe Czerniak. The tournament was over, and we were scheduled to play tomorrow against Partizan, the leading club in Belgrade. The three weeks since we had left home had been quite pleasant, since in spite of the political tensions between our two countries, the Hungarian authorities had gone out of their way to be fair and hospitable. The party following the concluding ceremony had gone on and on, and, a little tired, I was finding the monotony of the train's motion relaxing. The landscape was flat and very green, and, leaving the city that still bears the scars of the 1956 uprising, I welcomed the change. Having tracked the Danube for some time, the train was now following a different route. The Russian delegation was in the next compartment, and the Bulgarians, Yugoslavs, and Romanians were also on the train. Many of them were professionals, and they passed the time analyzing their tournament games. I had had enough of chess for the time being, and this sort of lazy daydreaming suited me just fine.

Suddenly the train started to slow down, although there was no city in sight. We were approaching Subotica, the border between Hungary and Yugoslavia. The train stopped, and several policemen boarded. As I prepared to present my passport for inspection I was very tense. After what felt like an eternity they finally came into our compartment, collected our passports, and left. I saw two of them entering a small office and didn't understand what was going on. Like me, Czerniak appeared to be disturbed. The policemen returned in force and commanded the six of us to take our luggage and get off the train. They shouted in Hungarian, and although with the exception of myself nobody knew the language, the meaning was obvious.

"Schnell! Schnell!" one of them added in German, anxious to let the train proceed as soon as possible.

We got off with our luggage and were immediately pushed inside a small room. The doors closed behind us, we heard the key locking us in, and, dazed by the implications of what was taking place, we heard the dispatcher blowing his whistle and the train departing.

So it had finally happened. Ever since the idea of sending a delegation to the Chess Olympics had first surfaced, many had cautioned us against possible harassment, or even imprisonment, once we were in Hungary. Throughout the tournament, there had been little to give credence to this pessimistic assessment, but now it appeared as if it had all been staged to catch us at the very last moment, just before we crossed the border. Here we were, shut in a small room, with no passports and no train. There weren't even real windows, only some openings near the ceiling.

After we had gotten over the initial shock, we sat on our suitcases and tried to make sense of things. We could hear the guard pacing in front of the building, occasionally stopping near the heavy door, perhaps listening to our voices, though certainly unable to understand anything that was said in muted Hebrew. Throughout our stay in Hungary we had been cautioned always to assume the presence of hidden microphones and to speak freely only in the open, and even then only if absolutely necessary. Our ambassador had given us his briefing after walking with us in the gardens of the embassy and stopping under a particular tree, a spot that was known to be clean of listening devices. After a few days in the hotel room we became less cautious and would give long speeches addressed directly to the unseen microphone. "Listen, microphone," we would say, "you must hear this joke." Sometimes we would curse it in Arabic. Now, shut away in this inhospitable room that had known better times, we assumed that it was bugged.

Moshe Czerniak, not so young anymore, was particularly distraught. Our ambassador to Yugoslavia would be waiting for us at the station and would not understand why we were not on the train. And what about the games tomorrow? It had taken a great deal of persuasion and his personal contacts to arrange this match, and now it all seemed to have been for nothing. I found it unbelievable that Czerniak could worry about such trivialities, but I later learned that this is a very useful method of coping. By concentrating on the trivia, he was acting as if we were still operating under normal circumstances. Being in charge, he must have felt the burden of responsibility weighing heavily upon him, and he was trying to convince us that it must have been a mistake of some sort, and that if only we could communicate with our ambassador in Budapest or notify the representative of the Communist Party in charge of the tournament, all would be well. But, given our situation, this sort of talk sounded rather hollow.

Every hour or so we would hear a train stop at the station and would listen carefully, hoping that it had brought the resolution to our problem. As each train left and nothing happened, we became more and more worried. But what was our problem? Had we done something wrong, or was this a purely Kafkaesque situation?

These were difficult times for the Jewish community in Hungary, since many of its members had supported the failed 1956 uprising. We had been explicitly warned not to establish any personal contact with local Jews or to take anything from them, since that might endanger both parties. "Beware of undercover agents who act as provocateurs; that is a sure way of ending up in prison," we were told. I recalled a man accosting me after dinner at the hotel, begging me to take a small gift to his family in Israel. "Don't be afraid, I am not an agent," he said, and his obvious fear underscored his claim. But we were forbidden to do anything that might compromise us, and after some hesitation I resisted. I felt the shame and the humiliation of being placed in such a bind. Could it be that one of my colleagues had been more forthcoming? Had we fallen into a trap?

In the windowless room, we put several suitcases one on top of the other, and with some help I climbed to one of the small openings near the ceiling to look outside. Facing the rear of the station, I could see only some small houses in the distance and several geese trotting by. And then, just as I was about to climb down, the smell hit me. It was the wonderful smell of sun-baked mud, and it was everywhere. The breeze carried it confidently and steadily toward the tiny opening where I stood, unable to comprehend its power and unwilling to let it go.

"What do you see there?" they all asked.

"Nothing, just a few houses and some geese," I said, and I let them help me down.

Later, when they began playing blindfold chess in order to pass the time, I thought of my mother in Jerusalem waiting to hear from me. It had been just before we had said goodbye that she had thrown me a bombshell: "I am so glad that you are going to that part of the world."

"But why?" I asked, knowing only too well the deep sadness that descended upon her every time she dared to reminisce.

"Your name may appear in the newspapers or on the radio, and, who knows, maybe Apuka is still alive somewhere, and he may see or hear it, and then he will know that we are here in Israel, and he might find us."

This was said very quietly and without a hint of drama. It had now been fifteen years since she had last seen him in Auschwitz, and in spite of all the evidence to the contrary, she was still waiting for him to find us. Could it be true? Was this why she had never remarried? Was this why for quite some time she had not wanted to leave communist Czechoslovakia and come with me to Israel? But she had never before mentioned this, even as a remote possibility. And what about the stories told by survivors describing Apuka's death? True, as with millions of others, the absence of a body that could be seen and touched and buried encourages hope to linger on for a while longer. But after all these years, how could she possibly think that he was still alive? Oh, Mother, oh, dearest Anyuka, not even Penelope would have waited so faithfully if she had last seen Ulysses in Auschwitz.

I couldn't find anything to say, so I had just embraced her and, fearful of parting, had quickly said goodbye and left. Now, sitting on my suitcase, the exciting smell of drying mud still in my nostrils, I saw her as she had been when she had confided in me, and I missed her.

It was then that we heard the key slowly turning in the lock and, after what seemed a long pause, the heavy door opened slightly. Through it came an ancient woman in a black peasant dress. Trembling, she looked at us and asked in Yiddish: *"Vilt ir telefoneern?"*

The next moment, Czerniak and I were following her through the door. She pointed out to us a telephone booth fifty yards away, and the two of us ran like mad toward what we believed to be our salvation, only to discover that it was an old-fashioned phone, without numbers. As I wildly turned the handle, Czerniak held the receiver, waiting for a human sound to respond. The old woman, the huge key in her hand, was motioning us to be quick. Finally someone answered, and Czerniak responded by repeatedly shouting the name of a communist functionary. This appeared to act as a miracle rust remover, transforming the ancient telephone system into a highly efficient communications network. The man was actually there, and after some more shouting about "diplomatic outrage," "Chess Olympics Committee," "international incident," and so on, we were told that the problem would be taken care of. We quickly went back through the door, and the ancient woman (where did she come from?) locked us back in, not even allowing us time to thank her. Breathlessly we speculated about what would happen next.

We did not have to wait long to find out. After a few

minutes the sound of marching soldiers could be heard, the door opened, and an officer—a new one, whom we had not seen before—saluted us and told us in broken Serbian that he would now take good care of us and that we would be put on the next train to Belgrade, due in at midnight. Eager to make our stay in Subotica as pleasant as possible, he mounted his old bicycle and rode to the village to fetch some fresh bread and Hungarian salami, and, more important, an old Gypsy with his violin. And so we spent several hours in this godforsaken place listening to beautiful Gypsy music, eating freshly baked bread, and, with the door now wide open, inhaling the wonderful smell of freedom.

FIRST MEMORY. The Danube in Bratislava. Hundreds of picnickers dotting the southern bank in Petrzalka. Apuka has spread a large blanket on the ground for all of us to sit on. The sun is hot, and a few adventurers enter the cold, swift river, only to quickly exit a few yards downstream. I am about four years old, chubby, and do not yet wear glasses. Suddenly I am lost among the multitude of similar-looking blankets and people, and can't find my parents. The dread builds up and I start crying. The tears are salty and I lick as many of them as I can. Somehow I get to the huge bridge and start crossing to the other side. I stop occasionally to search the bank from above. The height of the bridge adds to my anxiety. . . . And then, almost at the middle of the bridge, there is Apuka, his head shaved as it used to be every summer. He lifts me up, hugs me, and carries me to safety.

At some point I must have become too heavy for him, because Apuka put me down and took me by the hand. Although I liked the feeling of his huge warm hand clasping mine, I wished he would go on carrying me in his arms.

HALF A CENTURY LATER, in the complete innocence of lack of awareness, I wrote the following as part of my research concerning the various metaphors of hoping:

> Hope as a Protected Area.
> This metaphor indicates a situation in which everything is threatening, with the exception of a small area of experience that still maintains its positive features. Thus, for instance, one's health may be lost, all financial security gone, and everything falling apart, with the exception of one's family life. In this case the individual reports images of a small island of peace surrounded by storms and disasters. The work of hoping concentrates on efforts to protect the island from being overwhelmed by the surrounding calamities. The images often contain attempts to erect a protective fence around the remaining positive elements in order that they not succumb to the onslaught of misfortune.
> The wisdom of language, as a symbolic product of lengthy cumulative experience, is often quite striking. The Oxford English Dictionary lists many variations of the word "hope" as it refers to the

anticipation of a positive future. To my surprise,
the very same word, that is HOPE, is listed as having the following meanings:

1. A piece of enclosed land, e.g., in the midst
of marshes or wasteland.

2. A small enclosed valley.

3. An inlet, small bay, haven.

It is quite impressive to observe that all three
of these definitions actually describe the metaphor
of hoping as a protected area, and I find it hard to
believe that this is purely a coincidence. Furthermore, English is apparently not the only language
in which this happens. In Hebrew, too, the words
for hope and for a small enclosure derive from the
same root. . . .

The protective embrace of a parent, when the
child is distressed, may well serve as the prototype
for this metaphor. The child experiences, in con-
crete terms, that even though everything "out
there" is frightening or dangerous, all is still fine
within the protective embrace of the parent.

BOTH THE EMOTIONAL excitement and the spe-
cific content of my getting lost near the river fit well our
present knowledge of the nature of one's earliest memories. This is in marked contrast to my second distinct memory, which defies the more obvious explanations.

It was an autumn afternoon, and my mother was pushing my stroller. We were in Bratislava, near the Manderlak,
the tallest building in town. I was sitting in my stroller and
watching the street. Just before the entrance to the Mander-

lak, on the left, there was a tall gray wall. As we passed by, I was suddenly overwhelmed by sadness. The wall was so gray, there was nothing to look at, and everything was sad and boring. (I recall thinking that everything was sad and boring, but at the age of four, what could I have meant by "everything"?) I was struck by my own feelings and decided to remember this moment for as long as I lived.

I have made similar decisions on numerous occasions, with mixed success. (How does one know of a failure?) In this particular case, however, the task was clearly accomplished, for I have often evoked this fleeting memory over the years. Since it survived this far, it is now too late to forget it. Although each subsequent recollection almost inevitably introduced some distortion into the original, this fleeting state of mind has served as my prototypical experience of alienation—the perfect counterpoint to the drama of lost-and-found.

MY MOTHER USED TO TELL the story of my first year of life. I was a colicky baby and would not let her or the nanny (for those were still the "good times") sleep for almost a full six months. Nothing they tried helped; I was an "impossible" baby. The sound of my nocturnal crying became such an integral part of the household that one night my mother suddenly awoke to the unbelievable and frightening sound of silence. This was so unexpected that she was sure something terrible must have happened. Rushing to my room in fear, she found me awake, my eyes wide open, watching the full moon glistening in the clear winter sky.

"It was as if you were hypnotized," she would tell me. "And from that night on, you stopped crying."

I liked to listen to her telling this story over and over again, particularly the way she said "hypnotized" and the deep breath she took before the punch line concerning my miraculous transformation. It signaled my transition, and acceptance, into the category of "good" babies. However, the most wonderful thing about this story was that it put me in close touch with something that would serve as a pleasant reminder for many years to come. Whenever I saw a full moon, I would recall my mother's tale. It provided a special intimacy between us.

The moon story out of the way, she would tell me about the time I was supposed to die. I was barely one year old and had been taken to the hospital, where they diagnosed double pneumonia. This being before antibiotics, there was no treatment. The fever could be reduced, but the patient was required to "pull through" by relying on his own means. As the illness progressed, my condition suddenly worsened by my contracting measles as well. The fever would not go down, and I could barely breathe. It was obvious that I was dying. My mother was advised to take me home, as there was nothing more the doctors could possibly do. It would be easier for the family if I died in my own room.

She refused and insisted that they keep on changing the obviously inadequate cold compress to try to reduce the fever. All through the night she sat by my side (the story does not mention where the other members of the family were), watching my struggle with each breath, unwilling to give up hope.

As the night progressed, my breathing became increasingly more difficult, and then, suddenly, I stopped my fight for air. In panic, she called the attending physician, who to his great amazement found me, spent by the effort, sound asleep, the "crisis" over.

[MANY YEARS LATER, with our families by our sides, Judith and I found ourselves in a small room in the hospital on Mount Carmel, listening to Mother's final battle with death. The cancer had claimed all of her frail body, and as the hours dragged on, her breathing became increasingly more labored. This crisis was going to be her last. And yet, how odd that in the midst of this total hopelessness I was once again awed by the strength of her capacity for hope, without which our lives would have been very different.]

MY RECOLLECTIONS of Bratislava are very limited, since just as I was reaching the age when memory starts to play a meaningful role in one's life, we had to move. The situation in Europe was deteriorating daily, and Apuka thought we would be safer in a place where fewer people knew us. It had to be near the city, since his work kept him there, and he would come home on Sundays. Thus started the initial period of separation, like a prelude to things to come.

Our first stop took us to the famous resort of Piestany, and after the limitations of city life, it seemed to me like a dream. We rented a house not far from the glass bridge that spanned the river. It was a sunny place. We had a big garden with many trees. There were two walnut trees in the neighbor's garden, and a large part of their crown reached into our yard. When nobody was looking, Judith and I would pick as many of the ripe nuts as we could. They were very big and had a surprisingly soft shell that could be cracked by pressing two of them together—to this day my favorite method.

Apuka built us a swing, with a chair that could be removed and replaced by an exercise bar or two rings. It was summer, and I spent long hours swinging or exercising in the garden. Holding on to the rings, I would swing myself upside down and watch the garden above my head. Apuka was very athletic, and I liked to watch as he lifted himself up on the bar with his powerful arms.

For my birthday Anyuka baked a big dish of potato latkes, my favorite food. We used to celebrate birthdays on their eve, and since noon the smell from the oven had been spreading through the entire house. Later, when nobody was looking, I hurriedly gulped down several large pieces. This, my first memory of stealing food, was a precursor of a later unfortunate attempt to take a few potatoes from the nuns.

Around that same time, I was stung by a bee, and when the initial panic of the sudden pain subsided, I proudly showed my "wound" to anyone willing to look. Anyuka always warned us to be careful not to swallow a bee when we were eating jam; she was once bitten on her tongue, and it swelled so much that it almost suffocated her. It was a frightening story. Could life really be so precarious?

A day in autumn is engraved in my memory as one of

fear. The walnut trees in the garden were already bare, and so were the big chestnut trees in front of our house. I was coming home, and just before I reached the entrance I was intercepted by several geese, who would not let me pass. The lead goose (the mother?) was particularly ferocious, and every time I tried to sneak by she would extend her long neck, open her yellow beak, and, squeaking at the top of her voice, run after me, ready to bite. The rest of the flock followed her lead, storming me from all sides. I knew that a boy my age should not be scared of geese, but I was so terrified I couldn't move. Thus surrounded, I waited for help. It was getting cold, and I started to shiver. I had given up all attempts to get to the house and did not initiate any movement, yet the geese stubbornly stuck to their advantage and stayed put. Sometimes, after a long pause, the lead goose would try to break the standoff with a sudden threat, to which my only response was a defensive lifting of my foot and emitting of a meek cry. Terrorized, I now had tears streaming down both cheeks, blurring my vision. After what must have been a long time Judith, on her way home from school, found me in total despair. She laughed and took me by the hand. The geese made only a half-hearted attempt to hold their ground against the reinforcements, and finally I reached the safety of our home. It was on that cold autumn day that I first experienced the paralyzing effect of fear.

THAT WINTER WE MOVED on to a nearby small village called Vrbove. It was not something out of a Chagall painting or a story by Sholem Aleichem. Perhaps it had been, but by the time we arrived, any fiddlers that might

have been on the roofs of Vrbove had been taken to
Auschwitz. And yet a village it was: there was no running
water, and we had to pump it from a well, which worked
well enough unless it froze. Only the main street was
paved, and there was mud everywhere. Our new home
must have been very beautiful in the past, since it was built
like a small castle. But it was rundown, the plaster was
falling off, and there were mice everywhere. Apuka brought
a cat to take care of the mice, and I watched the pile of
dead bodies rise as they accumulated in the long alley. For
some reason this cat did not eat its prey but proudly
showed off the fruits of its labor.

It was a very cold winter, and to save money Anyuka
would heat only one or two rooms. On many evenings we
were invited to the home of the Kugels, who were the
landlords. They had a coal stove in the center of the room
that was red with heat, and we would all sit there taking in
the wonderful warmth. They did not switch on the lights,
and as the evening progressed the only illumination was
what came from the stove. Later, they would put some
potatoes on top of the red coals, and we would spend long
hours waiting for them to bake. The Kugels did not talk
much, and in the silence one could hear the sounds of the
stove. It was boring but very pleasant, and the blackened
potatoes tasted wonderful when they were sprinkled with
salt.

Each morning Anyuka would skim the fresh milk for
cream and collect it in a special jar. Once a week, on the
Sabbath, she would beat it, using only a fork, until it
turned into the most delicious whipped cream. I enjoyed
watching her hand working at high speed, and the trans-

formation was like a miracle. Sometimes she would let
Judith and me help her, warning us not to stop and not to
beat in reverse. It all looked very complicated. Judith and
I used to fight over each spoonful of whipped cream, and
on one occasion when I protested that she might have
gotten more than I, Anyuka, annoyed, replied that Judith
was one spoon older.

In the ignorance of childhood, I had only a remote
sense of the world that was crumbling around us. Although this, our third home, lacked many of the comforts
I had always taken for granted, we did not suffer. I liked
the snow and the mud and the well in front of our "castle"
and the baked potatoes at the Kugels', and I was crazy
about the cream. Apuka was very good at fixing things
around the house and was always busy arranging electric
wires, building shelves in the pantry, or hammering nails
on which to hang our family pictures. But the worry and
the sadness that descended upon him and Anyuka were
too obvious to ignore. By this time the rest of the family
had been lost, and sooner or later the Slovak Guards would
find us and take us away as well.

FIRST DAY OF SCHOOL. Shortly before leaving
for the city, Apuka took me aside and, looking deep into
my eyes, said: "Don't forget who you are, and always remember that you must be the best in the class!" And before
I had a chance to understand what it was that I was expected to do, and why, he was gone, leaving me with the
heaviest of burdens.

What was it that made him do it? Was it pure ambition? Or perhaps the wounded pride of the head of the family unsure of his ability to protect it against the onslaught of evil? The opportunity to find out was lost long ago, but not so the impact of these few ill-chosen words, which would stay with me forever. It would take me many years before I was able to mobilize sufficient resources to blunt their cutting edge.

Entry

Alone, alone, all, all alone,
Alone on a wide wide sea!

SAMUEL COLERIDGE,
*"The Rime of the Ancient
Mariner"*

FIRST GAME OF CHESS.

I have played hundreds—nay, thousands—of chess games in my life, but this one, at the age of eight, was the most important of all. My opponent was an older boy who was considered to be the best player in the orphanage. He looked pale; his head was closely cropped; and one of his eyes was almost entirely closed by a sty. We were sitting on a stone bench in the courtyard, and occasionally I could smell his sweaty shirt. Little did I know how like him I would look in a short while.

His good eye was also half closed, and he badly needed

a handkerchief. His smile was one of malice. The bench
was cold and uncomfortable. He opened the wooden box,
which when unfolded served also as the board, and spilled
the pieces onto the bench between us. Some of them fell on
the ground, and we both picked them up. The pieces were
quickly arranged. Then my opponent took a black pawn
and a white pawn and put them behind his back. I picked
black, and his smile now seemed more pronounced.

He was clearly unaware that facing him was a chess
child prodigy. This boy—whose name now escapes me,
although we spent a year together playing many games—
obviously hadn't yet heard about the tiny bespectacled boy
whose father used to take him to coffeehouses that served
as chess clubs and lift him onto a high chair so that he
would be able to see the board and watch him beat all the
adults in the club, and then lift him out of the high chair
and put him down and, holding his hand, proudly march
him out.

I liked these games against the adult players mostly
because of the chance to be close to Apuka and to sense his
pride in me. The coffeehouses were very noisy and filled
with smoke, and sometimes after playing several games I
felt dizzy and tired.

It had been when I was almost six that, watching several games, I suddenly picked up the moves, and then the
essence of the game. Chess became a lifelong passion.
Apuka was considered an excellent player, and he was
delighted to tutor me and to develop my talent. And yet
when he lost to me for the first time, I sensed some inhibited anger, which scared me. But that had been more than
a year before, and after it happened he stopped playing
with me and took me to the coffeehouses instead.

All this was unknown to my opponent, whose air was one of defiance. He must have known something else, though. For ours was not an ordinary game of chess but, rather, a sort of anesthetic.

Behind my back, slightly to the left, was a long dark alley that opened onto the courtyard, like the end of a tunnel. There, in semidarkness, were my parents and the mother superior, making the final arrangements for our admission to the orphanage. As I looked at the chessboard I was aware of the distant murmur of their subdued voices emanating from the dark opening behind my back. These were the last moments before the final parting.

Once the brief partisan uprising had been crushed and the Germans moved into Slovakia in force, our deportation became only a matter of time. The day before, Apuka had been tipped off by a friend, who told him that we would all be picked up the following night. It was then that our parents decided to put us in an orphanage, hoping to save our lives. All of us had converted to Christianity some time ago, indicating that this was an emergency for which they must have planned. Since early morning, Judith and I had known that it was our last day with our parents, and that tomorrow they would be taken away on a transport, and we would probably never see them again. There was no time for heartbreaking moments together, since they had to find a place where we might have a chance to survive.

THERE WERE TWO Catholic orphanages in Zilina, one with the Benedictine sisters, and one run by the Sisters of Saint Vincent. A few hours before, our parents had returned from the Benedictine convent disappointed. They had been told that the orphanage had already accepted several Jewish converts, and the sisters had even displayed the children, as if to prove that they couldn't take any more. That left the other orphanage, and after some initial negotiations we took some of our belongings and walked the short distance through the narrow medieval street from our house to the convent. We didn't hold hands because there were too many bags to carry and we had to get there quickly, and preferably unnoticed.

The massive door of the convent closed behind us, and I was struck by the darkness, despite its being four in the afternoon. All these years I have remembered that on that day at the beginning of September 1944 it was four o'clock, as if this carried some significance. And when the time to part drew near and I started to cry, Apuka had the idea of distracting me with chess and asked if there was a player, and Mother Superior, the huge white wings of her hat flapping with each movement, asked someone to fetch this opponent of mine, and the next thing I remember was the flood of light in the courtyard, and I was desperately trying to concentrate.

He opened e2 to e4, and I quickly retorted with e7 to e5. Next he played his queen from d1 to h5. It was a childish trap. How could he hope that I would fall for it? Of course, I could not attack his queen by playing g7 to g6, as this would cost me a rook.

Behind my back, slightly to the left, there was a sound of quiet sobbing. I turned my head, desperately trying to penetrate the darkness to see Apuka and Anyuka just once more, but my eyes were veiled with tears and my opponent was urging me to continue playing. I quickly returned to face this purest and fairest of all games, where the imperfections of the real world have no standing. And yet the unfairness of what was happening in the real world managed somehow to penetrate the neutrality that governs chess, and I played g7 to g6, falling into the trap, losing the rook, losing my parents, losing everything.

[THE WORLD OF CHESS is basically a just one, and there is no room in it for luck. As such, it is a perfect escape, a perfect reality surrogate, and the purest of all addictions. Although I started out as a child prodigy, my achievements in chess would never develop beyond a certain limit. In tournaments, after an initial success against good players, I would sometimes lose to weaker ones for no apparent reason. This sudden loss of concentration, this blind spot—could it perhaps be traced to this first game in the orphanage? For chess is supposed to be a closed system, but, once torn wide open by the crumbling world around me, the gaping hole would not ever be closed.]

SECOND GAME OF CHESS.

The final parting was almost brutally short. We all knew its meaning, and no words were exchanged. The tears of the four of us mixed together on our faces, and even after they left I could still taste the salt on my lips. It was the only tangible thing that remained, and for a while I tried to distinguish between my mother's and my father's salt. I had never seen my father crying before, and it made a great impression on me. Shortly after we were torn apart,

Judith—now called by her Christian name, Vera—was taken to the girls' quarters. I was left to play more chess in the courtyard.

Did my official entry into the orphanage mean that I was now an orphan? True, my parents had left only an hour before, and they were probably still alive; but it was only a matter of time. By the following day they would be in the hands of the Germans, on their way to Auschwitz, and that would be it. Few things were as finite and as clear-cut as Auschwitz. This hated chessboard was not clear; viewed through my teary eyes, it looked familiar but fuzzy. The contrast between the colors was blurred, and the bishops looked like pawns. Each time the other boy made a move, I somehow managed to peer for a short while through the tears, but then everything faded again.

My opponent was now in good form. Observing my face, he knew that I felt lost. At first I tried hard to hide my tears, but when my handkerchief had become a messy wet knot and they were still coming, there was nothing I could do. He seemed pleased and that hint of a malicious smile never left his face. I could not think about the game, and whenever his pleasure in my pain became too obvious, my only thoughts were of hate. I wanted to harm this torturer of mine, I wanted to make him suffer. He was bigger and stronger than me, and his entire bearing suggested roughness. I could imagine him badly beaten, his hateful running nose bleeding profusely, and yet, staggering on his feet, he fights on. He must have earned his toughness in many hard fights, for, unlike myself, he was a true orphan. And he had no handkerchief at all, while I had six of them, neatly folded with the rest of my things in my suitcase.

Anyuka had folded the ironed handkerchiefs for me, probably for the last time. What would I do once the six of
them were dirty? I did once try to wash a dirty handkerchief to remove some blood, and it was awful. The dried-
out green and yellow stuff became all slimy and sticky, and
I could not get it off my fingers. A clean, ironed handkerchief, neatly folded in the pocket, is wonderful; it means
you are not an orphan.

My opponent was watching me return from the dark
alley, which was long enough to prevent the light from the
courtyard from entering but not to prevent the sounds of
our parting from reaching the courtyard. This must have
made him overconfident, for now it was his turn to make
a major blunder. I saw it immediately and realized that I
would have my revenge after all, although it would take
place on the chessboard, and not in real life. The plan of
action was obvious, and my only worry was that he would
give up too soon, cutting short my triumph. If I could have
been sure that he would have agreed to play a third game,
everything would have been simple. In the absence of such
knowledge, it was necessary to put the pressure on slowly,
so that he would maintain some hope for victory as long as
possible. This called for a large measure of restraint, which
I found extremely difficult to muster. The tiniest provoca-
tion—the slightest hint of a smile, the smallest gesture of
defiance, even the unnecessary turning of his black knight
to face my white king—could jeopardize my resolve and
lead to a quick, head-on attack. The need for self-control
suddenly cleared my field of vision, and for a moment I
forgot everything.

But this first relief after the earthquake was destined to

be short-lived. Recognizing that he was lost, my opponent smashed the chessboard with one sweeping motion of his hand, scattering the pieces in all directions. There was not the slightest attempt to conceal the intention of the act, and while I was still trying to comprehend this latest shock, he got up and left me alone to collect the pieces.

P R I V A C Y .

There was a fresh onslaught of tears, but this time out of frustration more than anything else. I was still missing a few pieces when Sister C., who was in charge of the boys in the orphanage, entered the courtyard. I had met her briefly when the mother superior had introduced her to my parents. She had a dark look about her, and I did not like the way she slowly nodded her head when she was told about this new addition to her responsibilities. The way she had suddenly arrived on the scene made me suspect that she had been observing me from some dark corner all this time and had picked this as the right moment for intervention.

"Come, let me show you your room."

There was something cold and ominous about her voice, which, since I was on all fours, trying to find the missing white queen, came to me from high above. I could see her dark habit almost reaching the ground yet not touching it. This remained a marvel for a long time, until I realized that the sisters had developed a highly articulate way of walking so as to protect their habit from making contact with the dirty floors. They did not make any abrupt movements. Their gliding walk, combined with the gentle flapping of the white wings of their hats, added poise and dignity to their bearing. (The use of a cane by the elderly, particularly in combination with a slight limp, is, while totally different visually, one of the few things that can produce the same effect.)

The hem of her habit brushed my hand. At such close quarters, there was nowhere to hide. But how could I leave without having found the white queen?

"Stand up and follow me to your room."

"Please, Sister, just let me find the white queen. She must be somewhere nearby." And with that I moved a few paces away from the figure towering above me, desperately searching between the stones. It seemed that I was to be allowed a brief period of grace; but the white queen was nowhere to be seen, and when I saw Sister C. closing the distance between us once again, I knew there was nothing for me to do but to dutifully follow her lead.

It was thus that I entered my new home for the first time. Desperately holding on to the chess set, which had now somehow become my precious possession, I followed Sister C. through a labyrinth of doors, alleys, stairs, and more alleys, worried she might slip from my sight. At one point we met a few boys, but though I was generally aware of their inquisitive stares, I did not pay close attention to any of them. As we passed by, they muttered to Sister C. a subdued greeting, which she acknowledged with a slight nod of her head.

In addition to the impression of darkness, which by now I took for granted, I became aware of a distinct, all-pervasive odor. It was a new smell, unlike anything I had experienced before. At times it was covered by other, more

potent ones, as when we passed near the kitchen. It was
particularly strong when we crossed the long dark alleys,
where the walls consisted of large stones. It had an element
of dampness to it, but something else, too. The dampness
smelled like the cellar of our old home, where we stored
the coal for the winter. I liked the dampness, but not the
rest of it. Nor did I realize that this smell of the orphanage
would envelop me in its perennial and yet invisible
clutches, day and night, and enter into my clothes, my
bed, the very pores of my skin, until it would become such
an integral part of me that I would not be able to smell it
anymore.

Finally, we reached what Sister C. had referred to as
my room, which consisted of a huge hall with about twenty
beds arranged in a row on each side, leaving barely enough
room to pass between them. The entrance door had no
handle but could be opened by pushing with the hand or
the foot, or just leaning on it with any part of the body.
When opened with a powerful push, it would overshoot
and continue to swing back and forth for some time. I had
never seen such a door before, and I wondered whether
the fact that it was easily opened and difficult to close
served some purpose.

The beds were all neatly made, and on the third one on
the left, which we now approached, I saw my suitcase and
two small backpacks. Everything was opened. The suitcase
was big and heavy, and I could not pick it up by myself.
Apuka had carried both mine and Judith's, one in each
hand. He was very strong, and on our way here he had
rested only once. Mother Superior must have asked one of
the bigger boys to bring my suitcase to the room. Now it

was open, and my clothes were all over the bed. It looked as if someone had been nearly caught in the act of rummaging through it.

Anyuka had taken great care in folding my clothes and arranging them in the suitcase, and I had not wanted anybody to touch them. By now, however, it was too late; the suitcase had been violated. While I was playing chess, some of the boys had had a good time going through my things, perhaps even taking a thing or two for themselves. As soon as the thought occurred to me, I suddenly became absolutely sure that they had stolen some things—many things—and in great panic I started going over the contents to check. Without knowing why, I was suddenly desperately searching for my handkerchiefs.

"When you finish arranging your things, come down to the kitchen for some bread." The cold voice again.

"But, Sister, they took my things! Please, tell them to give me back my things."

There was a pause before she answered my plea. I was on the verge of breaking down in tears once again, and the pause gave me some hope. I looked straight up to her face.

"You will soon find out that this place is very different from your home, and the quicker you get used to it, the better." And she left.

I was fortunate to be so preoccupied with taking my inventory that Sister C.'s parting words did not really sink in. At least, not then and there; it was only later—though not much later—that they became the central core of my self-pity. Right now the handkerchiefs were more important, and after going through my things several times I found four of them. The fifth, the wet one, was in my

pocket, leaving just one unaccounted for. Before under-
taking yet another attempt to find the missing item, I
looked for a safe place to store the others. Next to each bed
was a small cabinet, but there was no lock, so that was out.
Near the doors—there were two of them, one at each end
of the hall—stood a large cabinet with deep shelves, which
served all the boys. I could see the few dirty clothes, lying
beside an occasional clean shirt, all packed tightly together
to save room. That left only the suitcase itself, which I
might tuck under the bed. I looked under the other beds,
and there was nothing there. Either this was not allowed,
or nobody else had anything worth hiding.

At this point the doors on both sides opened, and
several boys came in. A coordinated attack? Automatically
I stuffed all four handkerchiefs into my pocket. As I braced
myself to face the intruders, I could feel the reassuring
pressure of the handkerchiefs against my left thigh. I was
struck by my own calm. Drained of all emotion, I felt no
fear, only sadness. The boys must have counted on my
fear, for their resolve appeared to slacken. Two boys sat
down on their beds some distance away, evidently wishing
to play the role of spectator. But spectators of what? Did
they want to physically harm me? Could it be that they
already knew of my Jewish origins? No, that was impossible! Mother Superior had promised to keep it secret,
while at the same time cautioning that, under the circumstances, it would be unreasonable to expect that it could be
kept secret indefinitely. I knew only too well what she
meant by "the circumstances." My safety, as well as Judith's, depended on how well I could hide my private parts
from inquisitive onlookers. Living together with them in a

single room, I would be under constant observation. I would have to find thousands of tricks to dress, undress, go to the bathroom, and wash myself, as well as to guard against the more obvious attempts to remove my pajamas, whether in a mock fight or under direct assault.

All this must have been going through my head, for when one of the boys suddenly shouted "Show us your underwear!" I was not surprised.

"Show us your underwear!" he repeated.

"Show us the color. Is it really pink?" a second boy joined in.

"It can't be pink. Only girls have pink underwear."

"Maybe he's a girl?"

"Are you by any chance a girl?"

By now they were mobbing me, the two spectators included. Suddenly it all became clear: rummaging through my things, they had found the set of warm flannel underwear so meticulously prepared by my mother. The flannel was pink. In fact, all my underwear was pink, and I had never thought that there was anything terrible about it. But obviously I was wrong. At this very moment I was wearing pink underwear, and it was only a matter of time before they would find me out. So it was not just the contents of my underwear that needed to be hidden at all cost, but its color as well.

Then the thought crossed my mind that the one might serve as a distraction from the other. Since the boys seemed to be obsessed by the color of my underwear, once they had seen it they might let me go. On the other hand, they might wish to settle the boy/girl issue once and for all. Or maybe they thought that only Jewish boys had pink un-

derwear, and instead of diverting them from the real threat
it might turn out to be a step in the wrong direction.

While I was still weighing the pros and cons of a
partial surrender, the boy who had started it all suddenly
grabbed my hand, turned me so that I now faced the wall,
and shouted, "Quick, lift the side of his shorts!" The order
was dutifully carried out by two other boys, revealing the
pinkness for all to see.

Their laughter must have distracted them, for I was
able to release myself, pass through the perpetually open
doors, and run. I ran without stopping through the dark
alleys, the numerous doors, the stairs. Suddenly, I was
seized with cramps in my bowels and terrible diarrhea.
Vaguely recalling having seen a wooden latrine in the
courtyard, I somehow managed to find it. The final sprint
was accomplished by pushing aside several boys who, following Sister C.'s instructions, were now starting to gather
in front of the kitchen. The latrine was all that mattered to
me now, and I prayed to God that it would be unoccupied.
It was, and, locking the bolt from the inside, I quickly
relieved myself.

There was no toilet bowl, only a wooden bench above
a hole, from which came a terrible stench. Inside it was
dark, the only light coming through the openings between
the planks of wood. Crouching there (for I was afraid to sit
on the dirty wood), I could see the courtyard, whereas the
boys there could not see me. For a moment, I was safe.

The cramps kept coming, and so did the diarrhea. It
was all dirty water now, making such loud noises that
everybody in the courtyard must have heard it. I could see
them giggling and pointing toward the latrine. After a

while, somebody shouted about going to eat, and they rushed toward the kitchen. The courtyard was practically deserted now, and the sun must have advanced beyond the tall tower of the church, for the light had become soft and weak. My legs hurt from crouching for so long, and I stood up. It was then that I discovered there was no toilet paper anywhere. The bellyache was getting better, so I could start thinking about my exit; but without toilet paper—and lots of it—I was a prisoner.

Some of the boys started to drift back to the courtyard, munching their bread. It was obvious they had not forgotten the newcomer who had already provided them with so much entertainment. Among them I saw my chess opponent, surrounded by several other boys, who were listening attentively to what he had to say. Soon all twenty-two of them would surround the wooden latrine and challenge me to come out.

Realizing my predicament, I desperately looked around again for paper—or something, anything—that might help. When the boys started calling me names I kept silent. That seemed to infuriate them further, and the insults gradually intensified in a crescendo:

"Come out, you coward!"

"Come out and show us your underwear!"

"Hey, girl, can you piss standing up?"

"Hey, rich boy, how do you like your new home?"

"You shit, stop shitting and come out!"

"Come out and show us your pink face!"

I remembered the clean handkerchiefs, and for a moment I considered using them. I removed them from my pocket and looked at them: the beautiful checkered pat-

tern, clean and ironed and folded ages ago by my mother.
No! Not the handkerchiefs!

Sister C. emerged from somewhere and, crossing my
field of vision, slowly approached the scene. The boys were
obviously afraid of her, for they immediately stopped
shouting and tried to blend in with the surroundings.

"Duro!" She used the rough street version of my Slovak
name. "Come out immediately!"

I did not respond, but she could probably hear me
whimpering softly behind the locked door. Coming closer,
she delivered her next order in a quiet, hissing voice: "Unless you open the door immediately, you will get a beating
right here, in front of everybody!"

She certainly knew how to scare me, but nothing,
nothing in the world would have made me come out.

After making some more threats, she had the brilliant
idea of calling for my sister. That was too much; the
thought of Judith seeing me in this situation was terrifying.
And so while one of the boys was sent to find the sister in
charge of the girls—for no direct contact between the sexes
was allowed—I tried to clean myself using my fingers,
smearing the wet yellowish stuff on the walls of the latrine.
I was now in a state of panic and was not thinking about
what I was doing. My only wish was to escape from this
trap before Judith's arrival. The painting of the walls accomplished, I lifted my pants and with shaking hands
opened the door.

In spite of the gathering darkness, Sister C. was quick
to see what had happened. With an agility that would
make me marvel on many future occasions, she uncovered
my bottom, leaned me against the wall of the latrine, pro-

duced a long thin cane from somewhere among the deep folds of her habit, and proceeded to hit me. The swishing sound of the cane was accompanied by her unsisterlike curses:

"You dirty boy . . . You miserable creature . . . I'll teach you how to shit. . . . Oh, you will see, I'll teach you. . . . I'll teach you. . . . I'll teach you. . . ."

She seemed to settle on this last phrase as the most suitable counterpoint to her expert usage of the cane, for she kept at it for a long time. And I, realizing that even in the midst of her explosion, and in spite of the opportunity provided by the moment, she didn't call me a "dirty Jew," felt oddly relieved. Leaning against the wall of the latrine that bore my signature, exposed to all, I had finally completed my entry.

Lessons in Cruelty

"Fear is the parent of cruelty."

J. A. FROUDE,
Party Politics

FIRST LESSON.

I have learned a great deal about cruelty, but, oddly enough, very little of it was from being its target. The pain and fear experienced by the victim are relatively banal and provide but limited insight into the perpetrator's mind. They also monopolize attention to a degree that limits the ability to observe. Consider the almost prototypical simplicity of the following episode.

It was a cold winter afternoon; the darkness descended early and quickly. I was on my way back from school to the orphanage, when suddenly I felt strong hunger pangs. Judging by their intensity, the all-too-familiar stomach contractions must have been there for some time already, but I was too busy with other things to notice.

The way back from school was always full of danger. There were several boys in my class who competed to see who could make my life most miserable, and the icy snow provided them with many opportunities. They could throw heavy ice balls at me, or simply push them inside the back of my shirt. Fresh snow was less menacing, since its novelty provided a distraction, and they often found other games to play. Going to school was also complicated, but if I timed it so that I arrived at the very last moment, they could not do much. Frustrated in this fashion, they would still manage to threaten me with what awaited me during recess, or, better still, after school.

That day wasn't too bad coming back from school; there were numerous passersby not far from the school, and I could mingle with them for some protection. That worked well until I was a few blocks away from the orphanage, at which point I started to run. Two of the gang pursued me, but I did not see them anymore after I turned the corner. Obviously, they had found something more interesting to do. Finally I could relax, and it was then that my hunger began to assert itself.

It was a familiar feeling, and there was little I could do about it. My belt was already at its last notch, actively pressing my stomach. I had no money—with the exception of the oldest boys, nobody at the orphanage ever had any money—so buying something to eat was out of the question. There was the inevitable thought of stealing food, but I quickly rejected it. Strange how some forbidden thoughts lurk in the shadows, awaiting their opportunity. As a devout Catholic, I knew that stealing was a sin—one that I had had to confess to on several occasions. My last Communion had been only a few days ago, and I wished to protect my "cleanliness" and "innocence" for as long as possible. Besides, food was always well guarded, and the opportunities for stealing were extremely rare. As I turned the last corner before reaching the town square, where the orphanage was located, I recalled the one opportunity that had presented itself.

Several weeks ago, while on kitchen duty with the only other Jewish boy, Rudo, I had taken a moment off from the endless task of peeling potatoes to go to the bathroom. The kitchen was on the ground floor, facing the yard; our quarters were on the first floor; and the sisters' facilities were on the second. I don't think I had ever been to the second floor; certainly we were not allowed to go there. It was noon, and everyone but the two of us on kitchen duty was either in school or in the chapel. Although cold, the day was bright, the sunshine trying to penetrate the long dark alleys of the convent.

I could already smell the delicious aroma of fried potatoes when I was halfway up the stairs. Having reached the entrance to our section, I saw the pan of wonderful hot brown potatoes lying on the steps leading to the second floor. The potatoes, neatly cut and well browned, were meticulously arranged in rows. It had been a long time since I had seen anything like it. The sister who had left it there must have been in a hurry, or else the pan had been too hot to hold. In any case, there it was, and there I was admiring the sight, intoxicated by the smell, hungry as usual, tempted, resisting for a while. My heart racing, as if it already knew what would follow, I took the brownest of them all, swallowing so quickly that the taste was lost, my tongue burnt in the process, and I ran for my life.

The father confessor insisted on knowing all the details that formed the context of my temptation. For some reason he put great emphasis on the smell, as if that were the Devil's chief weapon. Ten Our Fathers and ten Hail Marys later, I felt the heavy burden lifting, making me once more worthy of salvation. More important, however, I could again pray for the safe return of my parents with some confidence.

Since that time I had often thought about the whole episode, perhaps dwelling on the potatoes themselves more than I should have. Today was no exception, and the images appeared to be controlled by my hunger rather than by myself. I frequently daydreamed about food, but not the wonderful dishes prepared in our home, which haunted me during the first months at the orphanage. As time went by, the dishes I thought of became simpler. I especially thought about bread. The smell of fresh bread, the sound of breaking the crust, the warmth of the loaf as it was carried from the bakery, and the heavenly taste of baked dough, somewhat sour from too much yeast. I comforted myself with the promise of bread and jam that would be distributed a few hours from now. There should be enough for all of us, and with some luck I might get a slice. That is, unless Hans interfered.

Hans was big, twice my age, and German. Tall and slender, with pale blond hair, which for some reason he was not forced to crop short, like the rest of us. He had ice-blue eyes that made me shiver every time he looked at me. When he joined the orphanage, Sister C. put him in charge of our group. On most afternoons he would watch us closely, making sure we didn't fool around and did our homework and performed our duties at the convent. I didn't know whether Hans was an orphan or, like Judith and myself, his stay was only temporary, until the end of the war. If the Germans won, he would surely leave, and we would stay forever. If the Germans lost (and they must lose, since I was devoutly praying for that every day), then Anyuka and Apuka would come back and take us out of here. Hans, however, would have to stay. I hoped he didn't pray, as that might weaken the power of my own prayers. I sometimes considered God's problem and wondered how He could make up His mind about the Germans.

I remembered having seen Hans in our neighborhood in Zilina; a good member of the Hitler Youth, he used to play the fanfare. He had even brought his trumpet to the orphanage and would sometimes practice. He knew of my Jewish origins and did not hesitate to use his newly found authority to make my life miserable. He also knew about Rudo, and later, when Fisher joined us, he knew about him as well; but it seemed to me that I was singled out as his target. Forever inventive, he would discover new ways of hurting me, always conscious of protecting himself, in case one of the sisters should find out. He didn't have to worry about Sister C., however. She stood by him and often found pleasure in "disciplining" me herself.

It was very cold, and we were huddled near the stove. There was a shortage of coal, and we were allowed to light the fire only late in the afternoon. Now, with the flames starting to lick the coals, we watched as if hypnotized. The large room was dark, and the single weak bulb could not compete with the fire. Hans was in charge of the stove, and he seemed to enjoy this part of his work more than anything else. After a few moments, the newly generated heat could be felt warming our shivering bodies, sending signals of comfort and pleasure. Hans had ordered me to fetch the coal from the dark and distant cellar; after that, I managed to avoid his eyes and stay out of trouble. Now that I was no longer cold, the hunger had become really nasty, and I was delighted when the heavy door opened and Sister C. brought in the bread and jam. There were seven of us, and I quickly counted exactly seven slices arranged on the tray. I felt relieved but continued to watch the tray closely. After putting it on the table at the center of the room, Sister C. left.

The moment she closed the door we all jumped forward, but Hans was too quick for us. He positioned himself in front of the table, and we hesitated. He took the largest slice—the one I had been eyeing—and casually started to eat it. As he chewed his eyes passed from one boy to another, cherishing the moment. His mouth, by now red with jam, was twisted in a malicious grin. After the third gulp—I was actually counting them—he called on Jozo, one of the bigger boys, to pick a slice. That left five on the tray. A few moments later, another boy was given his ration, and so on, until there was only me and the last—and, alas, the smallest—slice on the tray. He watched me closely, his expression broadening into an open smile. The others munched their bread in silence, waiting for the drama to unfold.

"Come, take your piece," he said.

I approached carefully and extended my hand toward the prize. At the last moment, with total ease and confidence, Hans pulled away the tray. I tried again, and the scene repeated itself. The boys now converged around me, and I could hear their excited breathing behind my back. I realized that my chances of actually getting the bread were slim, but I couldn't help trying to reach for it. The small round table with the tin tray smeared with the remnants of jam was my arena; the remaining small slice of bread, the enemy. I had to get to it and grab it and devour it, whatever the cost. But if the bread was the enemy, what was Hans's role in all of this? Like an angry bull attacking the red cape rather than the matador I kept charging again and again, but to no avail.

After a while the audience lost interest, and so did Hans. Just when I thought that the food might be within my grasp after all, he came up with a new idea.

"You and Jozo should fight for it. Whoever wins gets the bread."

Although I stood no chance against Jozo, it was too late to back out. My rage, fueled by sheer frustration, must have surprised him, but it didn't take long for him to establish his superiority. The knee kick to my empty stomach was more than I could bear, and it was all over. Hans would not let me leave the room, and, curled in the dark corner, far from the stove, weeping silently, I had to watch Jozo helping himself to my bread.

This was perhaps the simplest type of cruelty. The perpetrator, like the matador behind the cape, was totally inaccessible. And the victim, not unlike Sisyphus, bound to repeat the banally abortive attempts against forces out of touch and hence untouched by anything he does, was virtually a soloist.

SECOND LESSON.

Cruelty is entirely different when we ourselves are the perpetrators, and thus it is my own cruelty that I now wish to write about.

IN THE TOILET. It is dark, with just a remnant of sunshine, about to disappear as a prelude to a long winter evening. The "restroom" is tiny, dirty, and smells awful. I am there with Fisher, and there is hardly enough room to move. I don't recall whether I interrupted him or whether we entered together, but I think it was the latter. Somehow I managed to convince him—or perhaps coerce him—to go there with me, in spite of his previous experiences. He must have known that I meant harm, and yet he could not stand up against me. Fisher is about my age—perhaps a year younger—he is Jewish, he joined the orphanage much later than I did, and he is scared. His eyes are frightened, and it must have been this terror that got me addicted to tormenting him.

Once in the latrine, with the door securely latched, I proceed to frighten him. It is an unorganized and unpremeditated effort, but that does not diminish its intensity. First I call him names: "dirty Jew," "swine," and so on. Next I threaten him, to make sure he won't dare mention it to anyone, and particularly not to Sister C. Then I proceed to other types of torture. Chief among them are frightening gestures involving bulging eyes and gnashing teeth. I spread my mouth sideways with my fingers and show the whites of my eyes at the same time.

There is little actual physical harm inflicted—only an occasional twisting of the arm or pinching of the flesh. The threat rather than its execution is the technique, and fear rather than pain is the goal. It takes only a minute, but if uninterrupted, may take much longer. Sometimes it drags on until Fisher starts to cry, and I feel sorry for him and promise to leave him alone, he promises not to tell, and we part almost friends.

I can see his eyes filling with terror and then, at a certain point, sometimes rather unexpectedly, make the transition from fear to sadness. Sometimes I lose my patience with the slowness of the process, almost suspecting that he might be enjoying it. When this happens I have to improvise to speed things up. I can hear myself thinking: "Come on, Fisher, for Christ's sake, start crying, damn you! How long do you think we can stay in here?" Once he starts to cry, the sense of his abandonment and desolation is so complete that I am frightened myself, totally disarmed and strangely relieved.

Fisher is the only person I can recall ever harming intentionally. That makes him very important, and I wish I knew what became of him. In the darkest of hours, coldest of winters, loneliest and most desperate of times, he and I formed a shameful and yet a strangely human bond. By being an almost willing partner to my petty tortures, he taught me a lesson in humility.

•   •   •

[SUDDENLY, I WONDER whether Fisher wore glasses. I am preoccupied with this detail almost to the point of obsession. Supposing he did wear glasses: did I ask him to remove them prior to our "session" so as to be better able to observe his eyes? Isn't this the stuff that cruelty is made of?]

THIRD LESSON.

My teacher's name was Matejcik. He was a tall and bulky man with a dark red face. With his booming voice and cane, his command of our class was total. When he used the cane it was almost exclusively aimed at the fingertips.

"Make a nice rose," he would say, and the pupil would have to put all his fingers together to form a convenient target for the cane. The pain he could produce by this efficient method was unusually great without much effort on his part.

"Now make a nice rose with the other hand." This would invariably lead to an inability to hold a pencil and write for several days. The rose system was much more effective than the "lift your shirt" or "remove your pants" systems, and I often wondered whether it was Matejcik's own invention.

He had a beautiful deep voice, and whenever I heard him singing I was enthralled by its resonance. Even when we sang the blaring Slovak national anthem, his voice stood out from among a multitude of others. He also played the violin, Gypsy-style. He could play anything, without music, probably on the first attempt. Besides music he liked teaching math, and I was the best in the class. (I was also the best in reading, but that was less important, unless there was a visit by the principal, and on such occasions Matejcik would often ask me to read aloud.) He enjoyed numerical puzzles and tricks, so, at least for a while, I was protected.

When trouble came, it caught me entirely by surprise. One evening, shortly after Christmas, just as I was passing in front of the Grand Hotel, on the main square near the convent, I heard some shouting in the lobby and paused to observe the commotion. I knew the Grand well, since Apuka used to take me there to play chess. Sometimes on weekends he would play cards there for long hours, and Anyuka would send me or Judith to bring him home. Just as I was about to continue on my way to the convent, the revolving doors moved and out came Matejcik. He was obviously drunk, barely able to stand upright. In a daze, he looked around and spotted me standing there, watching. In spite of his intoxication and the dim light, I saw the sign of recognition in his bloodshot eyes. It was only a fleeting moment; he quickly raised the high collar of his heavy winter coat and with great effort walked into the adjacent alley. Instinctively I knew that something terrible had happened, and that my life in school would never be the same.

[A T H O U G H T A B O U T coincidence: Everyone has his own, often frightening, story of coincidence. As I think of this fateful evening when I happened to be in the wrong place at the wrong time, I recall my own classic experience of coincidence. For someone whose professional life is spent in applying the scientific method as the most valid criterion for analysis, an event like the one I am about to describe mocks both rationality and empirical science when applied to one's personal life. At the same time, for reasons that I do not fully understand, there is something exciting, almost perversely satisfying, in the defiance of traditionally accepted modes of reasoning. Whatever the cost, and however trivial the encounter, for a brief moment we are lifted beyond our dreary selves.

It was the summer of 1979, and my family and I were in New York City en route to Stanford University for sabbatical year. I was walking on the east side of Broadway, moving north toward Eighth Street, looking for the American Express office. On my right—in spite of my being practically blind in my right eye—at the extreme edge of my visual field, there was something tempting me to look. It was a bookstore. The odd thing was that the window had only one book on display: Arthur Koestler's recently published volume *Coincidence*. It was a huge window, and there must have been twenty copies of the book occupying various positions, producing an aesthetically pleasing effect. Part of my interest was probably because I had exchanged letters with Koestler. Although sporadic, our correspondence went back many years, to the time of my return from India, when he had published his *Lotus and the Robot*. Standing before the store, I thought about him and the fact that I had never met him in person. Some moments went by before I left the window and started walking, but after only a few paces, for some reason I decided to turn back. My progress thus stopped, while I was contemplating what it could be that had made Arthur Koestler write an entire book devoted to coincidence, and whether I should buy it right now, an old woman passed behind my back. I could see her reflection in the window. A few seconds later I resumed my walk, just in time to see a huge piece of glass falling from one of the upper floors, directly on the spot where I would have been if something had not made me briefly turn back. The old woman, covered with broken glass and bleeding profusely, lay on the pavement in a daze.]

M A T E J C I K   C O U L D   N E V E R   forgive me for being a witness to his drunkenness. He might even have been thrown out of the Grand and although I could never be sure about it, he knew that I might know. The next morning I did everything I could to make myself inconspicuous. Never once did I dare to look him straight in the eye, nor did I volunteer an answer to his questions during math. All this time I realized that he was looking at me, perhaps even deliberately provoking me to make a mistake. We were often required to "sit at attention," which meant putting our hands behind our backs, chest thrown out, head lifted high, chin tucked in, looking straight ahead without moving our eyes. The morning after our encounter, while we were sitting at attention, Matejcik crossed my field of vision on several occasions, and it was difficult to look through rather than at him. I recall his ruddy face quite close to mine, cane in hand, stalking his prey.

In retrospect, I behaved foolishly. If there could have been some face-saving doubt as to whether or not I had recognized him before he had disappeared into the night, my strange behavior, my avoidance of all contact, indicated the opposite. Even having seen him, by acting normally I could have pretended that I had not. That, however, was perhaps too sophisticated a notion for a child of eight, although such things often come naturally and probably do not require much experience.

Survivors of Auschwitz frequently mention the importance of avoiding eye contact with the SS guards at all cost. The main purpose of this behavior was clearly to remain anonymous and not to stand out in the crowd. During selections for death, one's only safety lay in numbers, in hoping that the quota would be met by other inmates. Thinking of Matejcik, I cannot help wondering if there might be another reason for not looking, namely, not to be a witness, and thus a source of embarrassment to the perpetrator. Could it be that on that distant planet, Auschwitz, the same games of human conduct were played?

OVER THE NEXT several weeks, the tension in school grew steadily, and I could hardly bear it any longer. The subtle antagonism of the teacher to his until recently favored pupil changed into open hostility. Whenever I raised my hand to answer one of his questions, it became his turn to deliberately "not see." This would sometimes be carried to absurdity, when none of the others could come up with the correct answer. The rest of the class would watch in amazement as he patiently waited for some new attempt by those who had already answered incorrectly rather than turn to me. If even that produced no result, he would simply give the answer himself. It was only when he was

absolutely certain that I did not know—could not know—
the answer that he would turn to me, his red face close to
mine, voice booming. There could be no mistake about the
meaning of all this, and by my legitimately becoming fair
game, my traditional tormentors were greatly encouraged.
Not that they had felt inhibited before, but their boldness
in cornering me in every imaginable way was now limit-
less. I sensed that something terrible would happen sometime soon, but when the crisis finally came I was totally
unprepared.

That day, the classroom was bright with sunshine, a
rare and longed-for event, providing the perfect decoration
for the stage upon which my little drama was about to
unfold. There were four rows of desks five deep, two pu-
pils to a desk. Mine was in the second row from the windows, the one before the last table. I had the seat on the
left, and on the right was Jan. It was a popular name, and
there were several Jans in our class. This Jan came from a
rich family; his father had owned a delicatessen not far
from the railway station, but the war had made his enterprise as a butcher more profitable. Jan was always dressed
in clean clothes and even had a real wool winter coat. He
used only new books, which he carried in an expensive-
looking black leather briefcase. He had no friends and
always kept to the remote edge of the desk, as far from me
as possible. I did not mind Jan and his wealth; the only
thing I envied him was that all his books were wrapped in
colored paper. Mother used to do this for Judith and me.

Jan was privileged; perhaps in addition to being a
butcher his father was also a member of the fascist Slovak
Guards. This could certainly explain why Matejcik never

touched Jan. He could do as he pleased and get away with it. Most of the time, though, he did not do much; he just sat there at the edge of our desk arranging his collection of erasers and occasionally doodling with his fountain pen. All the other boys used either pencils or steel pens that had to be dipped in inkwells and were a constant source of mess. A real fountain pen was like magic; even Matejcik did not possess one. During breaks between classes Jan would be asked to show how his pen's pump worked, and sometimes he even let one of the bigger boys try it. Everybody knew about his fountain pen, and on this beautiful morning his sudden exclamation "Somebody stole my fountain pen!" had a tremendous impact.

It was not just the content of the message but its delivery that was astonishing. I didn't recall Jan ever having participated in class, or even raising his hand. Suddenly, in the midst of a grammar exercise, while we were loudly reciting all the words that were exceptions to a particular rule, Jan raised his hand, and even before the stunned teacher could respond he shouted his accusation, the high pitch of his voice carrying the message above the muffled singsong of the class.

We all fell silent and looked at our teacher. He appeared confused, as if uncertain whether to carry on with the grammar, discipline Jan for his disturbance, or put everything aside and address himself to the problem at hand. Finally he called on Jan to stand up and repeat what he had to say.

"Teacher, sir, somebody stole my fountain pen." This time he said it in a softer, more composed tone.

"Are you sure that you brought it today?"

"Yes, teacher, sir, I always bring it with me."

"Did anybody see Jan's fountain pen today?" This last question was posed while Matejcik moved down the rows of desks toward Jan and me. In a moment he was directly in front of us, looking down at me, his voice now louder and his tone more ominous.

"I repeat, did anybody see Jan's fountain pen today?"

Why was Matejcik staring at me like that? Looking up, I could see his chest heaving in excitement. I was trying to think but was unable to concentrate. Had I seen the fountain pen today or not? I thought I had, but I couldn't be sure anymore. Matejcik's bulk towered above me, shutting off the bright light from the window. His shadow covered me, and I was terrified, waiting to be struck down at any moment. Why was he waiting? Wasn't this what he had wanted ever since that evening in front of the Grand? Meanwhile, something strange was going on behind me. I heard whispers, followed by a nod from the teacher as indicated by the movement of the shadow, and then it was quiet again.

Finally he spoke. "Everybody open your bookbags, and put all your things on the desk in front of you. I shall conduct a thorough search for the fountain pen until it is found."

I felt relieved that he had spoken and quickly opened my own bag. Jan's father must be a very important Nazi, indeed, for Matejcik to make such a fuss. After all, stealing in school went on all the time, and nobody had ever seemed to mind before. It must be the father, unless . . .

As I proceeded to remove my few books and pencils and my crooked ruler and put them on the desk to be inspected, my fingers touched something unfamiliar, and I froze. It was the fountain pen. I didn't know what it was doing there. My hand recoiled from its touch and came up with yet another crayon instead. All this time Matejcik had been towering above me, as if he already knew everything. What should I do? Somebody had trapped me, and I was doomed.

Suddenly, the boy sitting behind me, a hateful bully, the same one that was whispering, spoke: "Teacher, sir, I think I saw the fountain pen in Breznitz's bookbag."

Why "Breznitz"? Why not use my first name, Juraj? What was it that was so hateful about me? I was a Jew, to be sure, but was I personally responsible for Judas's betrayal? Did I kill Jesus the son of God? Why the total and merciless hate?

"Breznitz!" roared Matejcik. "Remove all your things from your bookbag."

And so it happened. My movements watched closely by all the vultures, I slowly removed whatever was still in there until the only remaining item was the fountain pen. He knew it was in there. Everybody knew. And so, when the time to give up came, I grasped it in my hand, my face distorted, half in disbelief, half in defiance, and brought it up and put it on the desk for all to see. The desk top was not level, and the pen began to roll. I quickly stopped it and put it back, and it began to roll again. I grasped it for the third time and held it firmly, lifting my gaze upward for the first time.

My teacher appeared very relaxed, a smile hovering on his lips. He must have been pleased with the way things had turned out. With measured steps he navigated be-

tween the desks until he reached his elevated platform at
the front. He climbed it, surveyed the class at his feet, and,
turning to me once more, said: "Breznitz, you are to stay
here after class. Is that clear?"

I nodded my head imperceptibly, but he was not satisfied.

"Is that clear, or not?" His powerful voice boomed
without restraint.

"Yes, teacher, sir," I said softly, but audibly enough for
him and his audience to hear.

It was when attention shifted from the catching of the
thief to the grammar lesson, and I was allowed to recede
into the background and collect my thoughts, that it all
became totally unmanageable, and while "sitting at attention" and looking straight ahead into nothingness, my tears
welled up and then kept on coming, as if nothing would
ever stop them.

The rest was almost an anticlimax. I did not much care
when Matejcik asked me to "make a nice rose," first with
one hand and then with the other, the cane swishing long
before its contact with the fingertips. With my hands thus
numbed, it was with some difficulty that I removed my belt
so that he could apply the cane to my naked behind again
and again and again. He seemed totally absorbed in meting
out my punishment, and had it not been for his shame, I
am sure that he would have called me names and warned
me never again to dare spy on his drunkenness. The part
that really scared me was his intention of talking to the
mother superior about me. If he knew that I had been
framed and was totally innocent, he should not have
brought the mother superior into it. That was unfair. My

own mother would have believed me, but I could not be sure about the mother superior. I hardly knew her. He must have sensed that the pain was not what really hurt, and so he spent a long time talking about how the sisters in the orphanage took good care of me and how I had betrayed them. Like Judas, I thought. Just like Judas.

MATEJCIK'S CRUELTY was more complicated than Hans's. To this day, I don't know whether he had been a party to the plot against me or had only made the most of the opportunity presented to him. If it were the latter, would this make him a better person? And how exactly was I expected to behave in all of this? Had I shown enough surprise, disbelief, frustration? Was my sad acceptance a disappointment to the perpetrators? Had I spoiled their fun?

History

Time has too much credit.

IVY COMPTON-
BURNETT,
Darkness and Day

THE RULES OF THE GAME are being violated at
the very moment that I am writing these lines. The as-
sumption is that as one ponders events of some magnitude
that occurred in the past, the present is kept constant and
is of no significance to the enterprise of recollection. If it
were otherwise, then it would be impossible to maintain a
focus, a point of view, and perceiving the past—a difficult
task even under the best of circumstances—would assume
the quality of a mirage. One cannot ponder bygone times
in the midst of dramatic action. At least, I cannot. Memoirs

call for a particular state of mind—a sort of detachment and quiet. The present must be "cold" in order to allow the once-"hot" past, which has had many years in which to cool off, to surface, in a measured and reflective manner.

The interference with the enterprise of recollecting the past is particularly great if the present drama relates to important memories. This is precisely how early trauma operates: relevant stimuli in the present prevent it from remaining dormant and reactivate its powerful impact. That, however, is an entirely different type of recollection, and represents the stuff that psychotherapy is made of.

HERE IS MY PROBLEM: As I dwell on the fate of my family during those darkest of days in Europe, Baghdad Radio is boasting that Iraqi Scud missiles have turned Tel-Aviv into a "crematorium." That was their exact word, aired today, January 19, 1991. They could have phrased it differently, using any of a number of alternatives: devastation, misery, defeat, desert, wasteland, destruction, ruin, fall, havoc, or even fire or hell. But the word they chose, taken from the unholy vocabulary that dominated my childhood, was targeted to hit the most vulnerable part of their victims' souls, with a precision exceeding by far that of the missiles themselves.

It did not start today; for some time already, Saddam Hussein has been threatening the newly gathered survivors of the Holocaust with *chemical* annihilation. Touché! This man must know some history—at least in the crudest, most rudimentary sense. And yet I cannot help feeling that even the most terrible and sophisticated of gas bombs, whether mustard or nerve, are no match for the one and only Zyklon B.

As I try to erase the impact of these new threats so that I do not lose sight of the all-important "perspective," the thought inevitably presents itself that memoirs are a luxury that should not be undertaken under any type of duress. And yet it is precisely at such times that I find myself more appreciative of the personal dilemmas and choices that my parents had to face during those years.

My father realized what was happening in Europe; there is no way he could not have known. On the weekends, when he was home in Zilina, friends would visit our house to hear his analysis of the war situation. He had a huge map of Europe, on which he used to illustrate his points. (I developed a strong attraction to that map, and subsequently to maps in general.) He was regarded as a very wise person, and people thought highly of him and often asked his advice. Could it be that Hitler's conquest and systematic persecution of Jews came to him as a surprise? And if he knew what was in store, why didn't he escape with us while it was still possible? After the war, my mother mentioned that he used to talk about moving to Bolivia. Is it possible that, like many others, he simply could not believe that such horrors would be carried out by the most cultured of people? Was he, like many others, deluding himself? Did he find it necessary to deny the threat posed by his crumbling world in order to be able to go on living on a day-to-day basis? What are the limits of one's personal responsibility? Can one gamble on one's family? Or perhaps his type of wisdom was too analytical and too sophisticated to transform itself into personal decisions. Maybe he had too much time to think and, like Hamlet, discovered that "the native hue of resolution is sicklied o'er with the pale cast of thought; and enterprises of great pitch and moment, with this regard, their currents turn awry, and lose the name of action."

On the day my sister and I were taken to the orphanage we were offered shelter by Zelnik in a hideout in the basement of our house, where he had a small distillery. Father refused, arguing that in spite of the Allies' landing several months before in Normandy, Germany was still strong enough to keep the war going for a long time. He believed that one could not hide for any length of time. Perhaps on this occasion he had too little time to think, or was too touched by Zelnik's offer. Perhaps he did not want to put Zelnik in jeopardy. I shall never know how he reached this crucial decision that has affected all our lives.

It is difficult not to be struck by the tremendous power of inertia, of status quo, as the dominant force in important matters of life. Is it a sign of fatigue, or rather the ability to maintain some hope even in the worst of circumstances? The future, after all, never comes, and even the most somber of threats may yet evaporate.

I had never seen Apuka undecided; but, then, I had never seen him happy, cheerful, delighted, desperate, surprised, or determined. The truth was that I had not seen much of him at all.

WHAT IS IMPORTANT? Are the events in the Persian Gulf that now appear so momentous truly important? For how long? To whom? Will the families directly affected by the loss of life there carry this memory beyond two generations? How about three? I have almost no recollection of my grandparents on either side. Having been killed before I could get to know them closely, they are just vague and sad unknowns in the context of a single faded photo. For my children, my grandparents' specific fate is irrelevant; they can go only as far as my parents.

What is important? Is my story of any importance? Are there enough threads of universal attributes interwoven into the tapestry of those distant times and places?

Is it fair to judge importance by the test of time?

T H E S M E L L F R O M Zelnik's distillery filled the basement where our coal was stored. I liked that smell, and when I felt frightened fetching coals by myself in the dark cellar, its familiarity was always encouraging. What would it have been like hiding in the midst of that strong smell? I used to imagine the happiness of the four of us, forced to spend long days and nights together. Later, these images were hopelessly distorted by the impact of Anne Frank's diary.

Once, about two or three months after my entry into the orphanage, Zelnik came to visit and brought Judith and me a can of sardines. I was so glad to see my sister that, with the exception of his mustache, his own appearance eludes my memory. We stood somewhere where it was possible to put the can on a stone, and for a short while we spent the time savoring the taste of the outside world. Judith might have asked him questions about our parents, but I am not sure if she did. We were very thankful for this, his only visit.

Zelnik was a simple man. Why did he offer us sanctuary, clearly knowing that it would put him and his family in jeopardy? Was it a shining act of courage in the midst of devastated norms of human conduct, or (what an outrageous thought!) an irresponsible and lonely gesture of bravado in the face of the dismantling of values? What happens when circumstances refuse to allow a person to stay on the sidelines, and he finds himself thrust to the center of the stage where the drama of life is being acted out?

Christmas

Music has charms to
soothe a savage breast.

WILLIAM W.
CONGREVE,
The Mourning Bride

CONSIDERING THE ELABORATE prepara-
tions, I should have been quite ready for Catholicism. Ever
since we had come to the village of Vrbove, Judith and I
had taken private lessons in catechism and in the ways and
beliefs of Christianity. These efforts had become even more
serious after our miraculous release from the camp two
years earlier. I recall being taught by a Franciscan priest in
a dark brown habit loosely belted around his waist with a
rope. His oddly shaved head was bald on top and surrounded by a circle of well-combed hair, which looked like

the halo of one of the saints whose statues were all over the city. The priest was shocked by my initial ignorance, but, realizing that I was a true tabula rasa that could be transformed by his teaching, he immersed himself in his task with great enthusiasm.

The lighting in his room was very poor, and most of it was where I was sitting, so that while he could easily see me, he himself was barely visible. The room was overheated, and it was pleasant to enter it after the walk through the wind and snow outside. Halfway through the hour, however, the heat would become oppressive.

At first the priest insisted that all four of us come, but after one or two such family lessons it was only Judith and me, and later we took some lessons separately.

Anyuka explained that if at the end of our studies we passed the tests, we would be allowed to be baptized and officially convert to Christianity. Once we were no longer Jews, our safety would be guaranteed. This last part was a great source of motivation, and both Judith and I took our lessons very seriously. My exceptionally good memory was a great help, and I could soon recite flawlessly all the major prayers and several passages from the New Testament. However, nothing could have led me to anticipate that my memory would soon save me from almost certain death.

For our first Christmas, Apuka bought a tree and lighted it with bulbs of many colors. We lived in the town center, just across from the main church and the prelate's house, and from our window on the second floor we could see the huge Christmas tree that had been put up by the city, just a few yards from the entrance to our house. It was getting dark early now, and I would eagerly wait for the lights on the tree to come on. Many people came to see the tree, which was there from two weeks before Christmas to mid-January, and to stroll under its lights.

Apuka promised that Santa Claus would visit, and we hung our stockings in the window to make things easier for him. I recall waking up and hearing footsteps, and seeing Apuka tiptoeing to the window and stuffing the stockings with sweets wrapped in shiny red paper. I did not tell anybody and the next morning pretended to be greatly surprised.

[O V E R   T H E   Y E A R S , I have often used the following vignette to illustrate the sensitivity of character formation to the minutest details of experience: Two identical twins are raised alike. They dress the same, and are treated equally by their parents, as if they consisted of a single person. On Christmas Eve they are standing outside the closed door to the living room, where the decorated tree and all the presents await them. When the door finally opens, both look excitedly into the brilliantly lighted room. However, there is room for only one of them to look directly, while the other has to peer from behind the back of the first one. And from that moment—so the story goes—they were never the same.

I think I read this somewhere, and for some reason it was given a sort of royal treatment by my memory. And each time I tell the story to first-year psychology students, I actually see myself in Zilina during this first Christmas, looking from behind Judith's back into the room and feeling very excited.]

•   •   •

THERE WERE MANY presents, all neatly wrapped. There were lights everywhere, and I was reminded of the Hanukkah celebration two years earlier in the main synagogue in Piestany. Apuka had made a small blue-and-white flag with a Star of David, and together with the other boys I marched around, and the women started to throw sweets from the women's balcony, and we all scrambled to collect as many as possible. The memory is one of warmth and pleasure.

Our parents tried very hard to make our first Christmas a beautiful one, and when they were gone I would often evoke these wonderful memories. But they made me sad, too, and later I learned not to think about the good times so often, although these images would often trick me and find an unguarded gate into my consciousness. However, the only Christmas that really counted, whose lasting impact cannot be erased by an act of will or the passage of time, is the Christmas of 1944, at the orphanage.

ALMOST FOUR MONTHS had passed since the earthquake, and I saw Judith only rarely. The boys and girls at the orphanage were being raised to become priests and nuns, and all contact between the sexes was strictly prohibited. I was the only boy who had a sister in the orphanage, and once in a while I was allowed to see her. She was a striking beauty, and Fero, one of the oldest and biggest boys, was deeply in love with her. He asked me to transmit notes to her and to bring back hers.

In return, he gave me some protection from the rest of
the boys.

The way the day had started already suggested something special; even the usual wakeup entry of Sister C.
appeared more benign. Her standard invocation, *"Nech zie
Pan Jezis"* (Long live our Lord Jesus), was pronounced in
a more leisurely tone, and our sleepy response, *"Na veky
vekov, amen"* (For ever and ever, amen), followed suit.
During the morning Mass we could see the various prep-
arations for the midnight Mass in full swing. The chapel
was adorned with numerous branches of fresh pine, and
there were hundreds of new candles waiting to be lighted.
Even the perennial caraway soup, our main food for the
day, appeared to be particularly hot and thick this morning, and the slice of bread was fresh. It was during breakfast that we were promised that the boys and girls would
have the holiday dinner together, which produced great
excitement. There was no school, and as the day wore on
we were busy cleaning our room, taking baths, and trying
on the new white shirts that were distributed for the occasion. I was looking forward to the opportunity of spend-
ing more than just a few short minutes with Judith, even if
we couldn't expect to be alone.

Throughout the day I could smell the freshly baked
cookies that the sisters must have been preparing and was
hoping that some of them would find their way to our
table. The smell seemed to be coming from a distant past,
and it was full of promise. So was the fresh snow that kept
falling. It was going to be a white Christmas, and the
congregation that was coming to midnight Mass would be
doubly moved. After the Mass, before retiring, we might

even get permission to spend a few minutes outside the chapel, sharing the excitement of the crowd.

The anticipation of the evening seemed to have an impact on all of us, and for a short while we were able to push aside the constant bickering and fighting that was a permanent feature of our existence. Extra coal was distributed, and all parts of the orphanage were well heated. And so, as the evening drew closer, the feeling of belonging to this place, for the first time since my entry, wrapped me in a warm blanket of comfort and well-being.

Dinner was served not in the usual location but in a smaller, well-lighted room. A Christmas tree stood in the corner, and we were seated on both sides of a nicely laid long table. I could see Judith at the end, among the other girls. There was no direct contact, as several sisters were seated between the boys and the girls. Near each plate was a fresh roll, and as the prayers went on I could not take my eyes off mine. The rolls were well baked, and their dark crust was broken in several places. Gazing at it, I planned the exact point where I would hold it, crush it, and break off the crust. Rolls were not bread; rolls were family and security, the landmarks of normalcy.

We were singing Christmas carols. They sounded unreal; their simple and pleasant melodies were totally out of context in the midst of the savage war that by now had been raging in Europe for six Christmases. The birth of the Holy Child in Bethlehem, the magic star pointing the way, the warmth in the small and simple manger, the proximity of the animals (particularly the lambs; there were lambs in almost every song)—it was so wonderfully promising. I liked the songs and I liked singing. Matejcik had told me once that I had a pleasant voice, and on several occasions, particularly in the chapel, I would hear myself singing too loudly. Sometimes I deliberately emphasized some notes, trying to add my own individual voice to that of the group.

The singing finally over, we could start eating. My roll broke along some unexpected faults, and the crust fell all over my plate. Wetting my fingers, I scooped up the dark crumbs one by one. The food was delicious, and there was enough of it. For once there was no need to gulp it down quickly in order to be ready for seconds while they lasted. The potato soup had just enough caraway to give it taste, but not so much as to turn into the regular morning fare. By sheer force of habit I swallowed too quickly, and the hot liquid burned my tongue and the inside of my mouth. For a while I was desperate with worry that I would be unable to taste the dinner. Eventually, with the help of some cold water, the problem was resolved, and by the time we got the meat (*meat!*) I had forgotten all about it.

The pleasant feeling of warm food in our stomachs released our tongues, and, contrary to the usual silence enforced during meals, muted conversation sprang up at various points along the table. To my surprise, none of the sisters intervened, and even Sister C. seemed to be enjoying the occasion. Judith and I could see each other and smile at each other, but we were too distant to talk. I hoped that after the meal was over our chance would come. She looked pale. Her hair was cut short and parted on the side. She was clearly the most beautiful of all the girls in the orphanage, and I felt very proud of her. And yet her very presence in the room was confusing. In this Christian new world she acted as a bridge to the old world, the lost one. Being a part of both, I was saddened by the intrusion.

The plates were removed, the table was almost empty, and we waited for the cake or the cookies or whatever it was whose smell had been driving us crazy throughout the day. Suddenly the door opened and Mother Superior entered, accompanied by a German officer. My heart skipped a beat. She was smiling, and so was he. In his right hand he carried a large package wrapped in shiny red paper, like the ones seen all over the town during this season, like the one Apuka used for the candies he put into our stockings when he acted as Santa Claus. Judging by his uniform, the German officer must have been a general. Mother Superior led him close to the Christmas tree, facing our table.

"Children, the commander of the German garrison in Zilina is a devout Catholic, and he asked to spend this evening with you. He also brought you a nice present."

Still confused by this unexpected development, I watched him unwrap the package to reveal a large cake. The collective "Oooh" at the sight of the cake, which had a brown topping suggesting chocolate, brought a wider smile to his face.

"Please, Herr Kommandant, take a seat." And with that Mother Superior arranged two chairs by the tree, and they both sat down. One of the sisters commenced cutting the cake, and we watched the icing as it stuck to the knife. Then the door opened and two more cakes, local ones, without icing but smelling very fresh, materialized. Gloria! Christmas had arrived.

But for me the cake came too late; it could not change the oppressive feeling produced by the entry of Herr Kommandant. Must the Germans intrude even on this night on the tiny and shaky island of peace that I tried to carve for myself? Were they bound to be forever a part of my existence? And I had felt so good tonight; I had had such plans for getting close to Judith. Watching her eating the cake, I noticed her own tension. She was eyeing with great concern the high officer sitting under the decorated tree to her left. Yes, we were in this together.

The cake finished, there followed a prayer and then more singing. We didn't know that many Christmas carols, and we were singing some of them for the second time. One of the sisters would start it and then we would all join in. It seemed that the Kommandant was requesting the songs, and we dutifully obeyed. Reclining in his chair, he appeared relaxed and comfortable. Maybe there was no real danger after all. Somebody started to sing "Silent Night," and the slow melody, like a prayer, held us in the power of its beauty. When we finished there was silence; it is not easy to follow this song with something else.

The Kommandant leaned closer to Mother Superior and whispered something in her ear. After some hesitation, she asked if anyone could sing "Silent Night" in German. It would make our distinguished guest very happy.

My heart beat fast: of course I knew the words in German, having heard them from Anyuka on several occasions. As was quite common in Jewish homes in Czechoslovakia at the time, Apuka and Anyuka sometimes spoke in German when they did not wish others to understand, or when they had German-speaking guests. Both Judith and I had picked it up and could understand most of it. I think we might even have learned the German version of

"Silent Night" before the Slovak one. But the only time I had sung it was at home, within our family. And now that the commander of the German garrison was asking for it, should I sing it for him?

I saw Judith slowly getting up from her chair and advancing toward the enemy. The decision was no longer in my hands, and I rose to join her. Awkwardly standing in front of the medals hanging on the well-ironed gray uniform, we clasped hands and were finally together. It took a major outside intervention to bridge the faithfully guarded space between the two sides of the table. My sister looked at me and counted to three to coordinate our start.

"Stille Nacht, heilige Nacht . . ."

As we continued, the face above the medals became animated and totally involved in our performance. I discerned a very deep breath. The lips started moving with the words of the song, and I waited for the voice to follow, but it didn't. We were approaching the most beautiful part: *"Schlaf in himmlischer Ruh'."* This last phrase rose all the way up, and just as it was about to be repeated with a final downward closure, Judith gasped and stopped. She was not crying; her eyes were wide open in an expression of total surprise. She was too scared to go on.

I could hear our mother's soft voice in the background throughout the entire song, and I am sure Judith did as well. Had she broken down in an outpouring of sadness, I would have been immediately ready to join her. The emotion had been gathering strength inside my chest and in my throat, ready to burst. The point at which she had stopped was the one at which I would have predicted something might happen; the melody invited it. But why this fear, this absolute terror on her face? What dreadful thought had crossed her mind?

In the silence of the unexpected pause, punctuated by the increasing pressure of her hand on mine, in a flash I finally understood: Why was it that the two of us were the only ones to know the German version of this song? Where were the rest? There were no others because in this country only Jews (*Jews*) understood German. The person above the medals must have known this, too; after all, it was he who had trapped us.

Another deep breath lifted the medals, and both hands motioned us to approach. Betrayed! Betrayed! We moved slowly, aware that Mother Superior was suddenly standing and inserting herself into the small space where the next scene was about to be enacted. Would she save us now that we had betrayed ourselves? Could she protect us against Herr Kommandant himself? We were closing in and would soon be in contact with the hands that were still hanging in the outstretched, inviting position. I saw no way to avoid touching them.

At the last moment, both hands focused on my sister. As I stood before him, the face of the sitting officer was directly opposite my own. He raised his hands to stroke her head, and his eyes softened and there was the hint of a tear.

"Hab keine Angst, deine Mutter und dein Vater werden zurückkommen." (Don't be scared, your mother and father will come back.)

The message, combined with the tenderness of the delivery, was too much for us, and we could no longer hold back our sobs. While he stroked Judith's hair and her high forehead, she attended to me. Mother Superior tried to join in, but, realizing that all the major slots were filled, she abstained, and eventually she sat down. This took place behind my back, but in the stillness of the moment the rustling of her habit told the story.

Fear and sadness do not mix well, and in the midst of what started as a heartwarming consolation, the awareness that the commanding officer of the German garrison knew we were Jewish asserted itself. Total vulnerability. Tonight the homesickness evoked by the melody of the unfinished song provided some safety. But what about tomorrow morning? Once released from the orbit of that melody, other, unknown forces might prevail. For us, nothing would ever be the same as we awaited the conclusion of the story born on that Christmas Eve.

[FOR A FULL THIRTY YEARS, the idea of Christmas for me was totally dominated by these events. In my ignorance, I was confident that it would forever consist of a scene assembled from the following pieces: the orphanage, the good smells, my sister, the German officer, his cake, the carol, and the subsequent mixture of fear and wonder. Then, exactly thirty years later, without any warning, on Christmas Eve Judith had to take our mother to the hospital, where within a month she died. Memories of her dignified struggle with cancer, matched only by the frailty of her devastated body, have since taken over from those earlier images, occasionally giving way, and sometimes producing the oddest of mixtures.]

The Test

Hesperian fables true,
If true, here only.

MILTON,
Paradise Lost

IN ADDITION to the frequent Dominus Vobiscum, the Pater Noster, the Kyrie, the Agnus Dei, and the Credo, there were the endless Litanies. The sisters would read these prayers aloud in Latin while walking down the long corridors or inside the chapel or, weather permitting, in the courtyard itself. They were almost invariably walking, as if this elevated the action, which was basically automatic. It was obvious that, apart, perhaps, from the mother superior, none of them could understand Latin. At the same time, as in the Psalms, the words of these Litanies tend to repeat themselves. Even now, half a century later, I can recall the sound of the Miserere. It was a particular favorite.

I enjoyed listening to Latin. There was something soothing in the monotony of the voices, although compared with the constant repetition of "Om Mani Padme Hum" of the Buddhists, it must seem full of interest and even the occasional surprise. The suffixes did the trick: the "saecula saeculorums" suggested a pattern of orderliness that evoked a sense of well-being. My exposure to these protracted prayers for many hours each day set the stage for a story that I still find fascinating and unbelievable.

T H E   T E R M "eidetic imagery" is psychological jargon for "photographic memory." By looking at something just once, certain individuals can later recall all the details from memory, as if the original stimulus were still in front of their eyes. This extreme capability is very rare. The somewhat reduced version of having an exceptionally good memory is, of course, more prevalent. As a child, I was fortunate to have an outstanding memory, both visual and auditory. While the former helped me to read early and fast, and surely contributed to my chess playing, the second may well have saved my life.

It was the constant deterioration of my memory in later years that more than anything created an aura of disbelief in my own mind concerning the events I am about to describe. What came to me naturally and without any effort when I was a child now seems almost a miracle. However, the incredulity of my own part in the story is more than matched by its content, as well as its implications.

I AM NOT SURE who it was who first discovered I
could recite some of the long Litanies by heart. It might
have been Sister C., although I doubt that she would have
acted so quickly, rushing to Mother Superior for counsel.
And yet it could have been her, since she more than anybody else had access to us, including the remaining shreds
of private life we still possessed. My hesitation about her
role might well be based upon the constant ambivalence I
felt toward her. From the moment of my entry into the
orphanage, she had been guilty of endless attempts to make
my days—and nights—as miserable as possible, without
obviously overstepping her authority and seeming impartiality. At the same time, by virtue of our total dependence
on her good will, all the boys, myself included, made sure
to court her favors. Too much was at stake; Sister C. was
the guardian of our fortunes.

To complicate the issue even further, I distinctly recall
that her attitude toward me changed significantly about
the time of the discovery, and I am unable to distinguish
between cause and effect. Was it she who discovered me?
Or perhaps she drew her own conclusions about my new
status in the small community of the cloister, shielded
from the outside world by religion as well as the high walls
and the heavy, carefully locked doors.

Whoever it was who alerted Mother Superior to my
strange ability to repeat the long prayers from memory—
and it could easily have been one of the boys, who must

have noticed me talking to myself in Latin—placed into motion something that would not be put to rest for a long time. The initially minute interference in our lives by others—a priori insignificant and yet, once having gained entry into the innermost orbit, starting a small perturbation that can travel far and wide—remains a mystery and a major source of frustration to anyone attempting to interpret a biography.

I FOUND MYSELF in the chambers of Mother Superior—the very room where my father had discreetly negotiated our entry into the orphanage. It was reached directly from the dark corridor leading to the courtyard. I had never been in this room before, and I wondered why the later part of that negotiation had been carried out in the corridor rather than here. Could it be that they had been on their way out and something important had occurred to them—something too important for them to waste time on returning to the more private quarters? Was this perhaps the point when Mother Superior had asked what to do about us in case both parents failed to come back? Or if, in spite of everything, Germany were to win the war? It might have been Apuka who had suddenly remembered to mention a place where additional funds could be found to further help the orphanage in the future? Or Anyuka making sure that Mother Superior would take personal care of Judith, who might be starting to menstruate soon (the boys talked about this often in the evenings), or of my glasses, which might need adjusting a few years hence?

The room was almost entirely dark, and everything in it suggested austerity. Mother Superior sat behind an old, heavy table facing the entrance. Above her, slightly hidden from my view by the wide wings of her hat, was a small wooden crucifix. It was much smaller than the others found everywhere in the cloister; it was even smaller than the one in the boys' room. On the left, a picture of the Holy Mother and Child was the only addition to an otherwise empty wall. To the right, behind Sister C., was a shelf packed with books.

A gentle smile on her face, Mother Superior encouraged me to sit down on the remaining chair, next to Sister C., who for some reason was also smiling. When we had entered she had briefly held my hand, suggesting a close personal interest. The length of her sleeves made it impossible to hold her hand without coming into contact with the dress itself. The cloth, heavily starched, was hard to the touch. Now, sitting tense in front of her superior, she inserted each hand into the opening of the opposite sleeve, making them disappear entirely.

"I have heard that you have a very good memory. Is it so?"

Until this very moment, I had had no idea of what it was that Mother Superior had wanted to see me about. At one point I had even cherished some hope of hearing good news, only to be followed by fear of the worst. It was midwinter of 1945, and there were no signs of the war coming to an end. On the contrary; one could often see many German soldiers passing through the town on their way to the Russian front. Everybody talked about the Russian front, suggesting that it was there that the final outcome would be determined. I often asked where the Russian front was, but nobody seemed to know. By my reckoning, it could have been very far, indeed, perhaps in Russia itself.

When Sister C. came to fetch me from kitchen duty, my first thought had been that I had done something wrong, or that one of the boys had tried again to get out of a jam by naming me as the transgressor. It had happened so often before that I almost took it for granted. Quickly washing from my hands the dirt of the frozen potatoes, which were almost impossible to peel, I resigned myself to what lay ahead. But never before, even when Hans had spread lies about my laughing at some religious practices, had I been called to appear before Mother Superior. Sister C. was quite capable of handling all disciplinary matters by herself. So this must be something else.

What was this about my memory? In my embarrassment, I looked down at my hands, observing the dirt from the potatoes hiding stubbornly under my nails, not knowing what to say.

"Don't be afraid, Juri." (Oh, the soft version of my name—it had been so long since I had heard it spoken.) "I am not going to be angry with you." And, after a while, "Look at me, Juri." (Oh, again.)

Slowly I lifted my gaze to meet her kind eyes. The smile was still there, and as she nodded her head gently, the crucifix behind her came into full view, only to disappear again behind the mass of whiteness above those eyes.

"Is it true that you know some of the Litanies by heart?"

So that was it. As the heavy burden was lifted, I was overcome by a warm feeling of gratitude. Yes, she was everything that I had heard about her, and more. A kind old woman, an exemplary nun, a true Christian.

"Yes, Sister," I replied, emboldened. "I do remember some of them."

No sooner had the words left my lips than I started to worry. Was it all right to call her "Sister"? Should I have rather called her "Mother Superior," or perhaps just "Mother"? Was she insulted?

She opened a book of Litanies and started to read aloud. Then, after a short while, she asked, "Do you know this one?"

"Yes, Sister."

"Can you tell me how it continues?"

Out of the deep recesses of my memory came a surge of words in a language I did not understand. It was the language of my newly acquired belief. The words flowed easily, each encouraged by the music of the preceding one. Yes, and by the wonderful smile of this woman, so different from, and yet so similar to, my own beloved mother.

Suddenly overwhelmed by emotion, I burst into sobs, terminating the Litany in the middle. Through the prism of tears I now saw not one but several crucifixes behind the several heads of Mother Superior. They seemed to be dancing, unable to rest. Then several hands reached across the table and came to rest on the top of my head. Once there, they all combined into a single touch. I closed my eyes, squeezing the moisture outside. With the back of my left hand—the handkerchiefs were all long gone—I tried to wipe my eyes, all the time concentrating on the single touch of the many hands that were now gently stroking my hair.

"Don't cry, Juri. You did well. You did very well."

Another surge of emotion threatened to undo everything, but then the hands left me, and I managed to control it. Slowly opening my eyes, I found that the smile had been replaced by a sad expression that I could not understand. Where did it come from? And why was she raising her eyebrows? If they wore their hat too low, the sisters sometimes covered a part of their eyebrows, but this was not the case here. On the contrary, the whiteness of the hat going all the way down to the lower forehead contrasted with the dark eyebrows of Mother Superior, which now seemed to be the focus of her disbelief.

"How do you do it? Do you read it hundreds of times when no one is looking? Tell me, Juri" (now less soft, almost accusatory), "how can you remember all these Latin words?"

"I don't know, Sister." My voice was barely audible. "I don't do anything. The words just come to me on their own."

"Are you sure?" The stern interrogator.

"Yes, Sister."

There was a long pause, during which her expression changed once again. She was apparently satisfied that I was not cheating, and her eyes softened, and so did her voice. Turning to Sister C., she said, "I don't want anyone to know about this yet. I must think about what to do, and in the meantime we should keep this to ourselves." And, turning to me (I could not help feeling pleasure at watching Sister C.'s bewildered acquiescence), "You, too, must promise me not to talk about this with anybody. It is very important."

I could not understand the importance of the secrecy, nor did I realize what was happening. At the same time, my "Yes, Sister" sounded genuine, and without much ceremony, the interview ended as abruptly as it had begun. On the way out, Sister C. once again took hold of my hand, gently prodding my exit.

In the long, infamous corridor, the light coming from the courtyard was suddenly too dazzling. We walked toward it in silence. I could hear the rustling of her starched habit. And then, as we reached the courtyard, suddenly, without any warning, she said in parting, "I shall pray for you tonight," and she left me in my bewilderment.

A FEW DAYS went by, and were it not for the odd change in Sister C.'s attitude toward me, I would have regarded the entire episode as being a thing of the past. During our daily routine there were no opportunities to talk with Mother Superior; the only times I could see her were from a distance during the early Mass and more closely when I was ministering to the priest and thus occasionally facing the congregation. After the meeting in her office I became even more interested in ministering than before. Whenever someone was needed, I volunteered for the job. Not that there were many competitors among the other boys, since even the left altar boy had to remember a lot of details, not to mention the one on the right. A good memory was certainly helpful, since none of the priests liked to be put in the position of having to whisper their orders and remind the altar boys what to do.

For several days I had been vainly searching Mother

Superior's face for some clue; but she did not even acknowledge my gaze. One thing, however, did change: I became more involved with the Litanies and often found myself rehearsing them from memory. It was as if I realized that the real test was yet to come. When walking behind the sisters, I sometimes found myself straining my ears in order better to hear the Latin sounds:

> Kyrie eleison.
> Christe eleison.
> Kyrie eleison.
> Iesu, audi nos.
> Iesu, exaudi nos.
> Pater de caelis, Deus, miserere nobis
> Fili, redemptor mundi, Deus, miserere
> Spiritus Sanctus, Deus, miserere
> Sancta Trinitas, unus Deus, miserere
> Iesu, Fili Dei vivi, miserere . . .

Lying in bed at night, I often tried to recall a new passage. Sometimes, when nothing came, I would panic and search my mind in vain. Now that I had become aware of my capability, it appeared to be shrinking.

Then, one afternoon (everything was happening on afternoons), Sister C. asked me to wash, change my shirt, and be ready to go with her and Mother Superior to the prelate's house. Being the highest religious authority in town, the prelate lived in a spacious house near the main church, right across from what used to be our house. The thought of going *there* frightened me, particularly since I knew that our house was now occupied by strangers, and

I did not want to see them. In the beginning I used to sneak out of the orphanage and approach the house, perhaps hoping to see my parents back from Auschwitz. It was only under cover of darkness that I had the courage to go there, as I feared being recognized by one of the fascist neighbors, who might report me to the Slovak Guards. Then, one evening, I saw a young couple go up to the house; the man produced a key—*our* key—and in they went. They were a merry couple, talking loudly, laughing, and obviously enjoying life. A few moments later I saw the light in the living room go on, and the silhouette of the woman could be seen by the window. Soon she disappeared into another part of the house, and after waiting some more I left the scene, deciding never to come back.

Then there was the additional fear of meeting the prelate. Having been my neighbor for two and a half years, he would surely remember me. And what if he recalled the incident with the water? That would be terrible. As I was changing my shirt and combing my short hair, I went over that incident in my mind.

It was late afternoon (again, like the refrain in Lorca's "Lament for Ignacio Sanchez Mejias": *"A las cinco de la tarde / Ay, que terribles cinco de la tarde"* ["At five in the afternoon / Ah, that fatal five in the afternoon"]), and it was summer, and everybody was outside. A friend came to visit, and we sat on the balcony overlooking the busy street and watched the game of soccer in progress at the far end of the street, just before where it made a sharp curve to the left. There was no ball; nobody ever had a real ball, so the players improvised by tying some rags into a knot that would respond to a kick, though, of course, it had no elasticity and could not bounce. This imitation ball (*han-drak* in Slovak) was very hard and was responsible for broken windows on more than one occasion. Once the knot started to disintegrate from the kicks, the loose ends were painful when a player gave a head kick. There were only six players, including the two goalies. Once in a while a car would disrupt the game, but these interruptions were rare.

After a while we became bored with watching the un-eventful game and tried to come up with something more interesting to do. My friend suggested that we spill water on unsuspecting passersby who were strolling under the window. At first I was hesitant, since he would be going home while I would be staying to face the storm; but after some pressure I agreed and proceeded to provide a glass, a pitcher, and finally a bucket full of water. So prepared, we waited for a suitable victim.

This was exciting. Several neighbors went by, and I had a hard time restraining my friend from premature action. Although we agreed we should not select someone who knew me, I kept hoping that one of the neighborhood girls would come by—perhaps even Marina, who lived across the street and whom I liked to watch. After a few minutes of tense waiting we saw a teenaged boy approach-ing the trap. When he was almost clear of the window I emptied the glass, and even before we could see what had happened the two of us dashed inside the house. A few seconds later we ventured to peek out, only to see the boy crossing the street without even looking back. It was dif-ficult to decide whether it was a total miss or a total suc-cess. Nobody seemed to notice, and thus emboldened I emptied the newly filled glass when a peasant woman carrying some homemade butter wrapped in big green leaves entered the danger zone. We ducked again but emerged soon, in time to see her wiping her face with a kerchief that she must have removed from her now loose hair. This done, she cast one glance in our direction, smiled softly, and went on her way.

In hindsight, I realize that had she gotten angry and cursed, everything would have ended reasonably well. It was precisely her acceptance of our prank that turned out to be my undoing. For soon after she turned the corner we saw the prelate himself walking on our side of the street. He presented an impressive sight: his long robe was blue and scarlet, the scarf gold. His robe was gathered at his waist with a wide black satin belt. And, most important to our story, his head was crowned by a magnificent wide hat, also black, with a scarlet band surrounding the halo of the circumference. The hat was so big that it was impossible to miss, even from the height of the window. Before I could stop him, my friend, who until now had been content with being a passive spectator, lifted the bucket itself and emptied its contents on top of the irresistible target.

In my shock, I did not dare leave the false security of the room to see what had happened. There was a commotion outside, and several neighbors came out to participate in the excitement of the incident. My friend—if he could still be called that—became strangely silent. Coming from a respected Catholic family, he suddenly realized what it was that he had done. However, this did not prevent him from peering out and reporting back that the hat, heavy from all that water, had collapsed downward and covered the prelate's face. He then ran down the stairs and out into the yard of Zelnik's distillery. From there he must have found a way to escape without going into the street.

For a Jewish child to insult the highest Christian authority in town was not a small matter even during so-called normal times, if ever there were such. On this summer day of 1943, it was suicidal.

The waiting for all hell to break loose was the most difficult part. Several hours went by; it was already getting dark outside; and yet nothing had happened. My mother came home and saw me hiding in my room, but I could not bring myself to tell her. It was not that I believed I could get away with it, but the thought of informing her about my endangering the entire family—for that much I now understood—was simply too frightening.

When the doorbell finally rang, I rushed to the bathroom and without switching on the light locked myself in, sitting in darkness (why?) as I listened to the ominous muffled voices. When Judith asked me to come out and face the firing squad I did not even answer, as if they did not know where I was hiding. She pleaded with me, but without success. Next I heard my mother, her voice on the verge of breaking, begging me to come out and tell my side of the story. I was tempted to tell on my friend but realized that nobody would believe me, and even if they did, I was still the responsible party. At this point I was committed to silence, and I stayed put. Some more subdued discussion, and finally the visitor (or visitors) took his leave.

Suddenly it became very quiet, and I did not know what to make of it. Then the lights in the living room went out, and after a while I tried to sneak into my bed, thankful that it was only Tuesday, and my father would not be coming home until Saturday. Between now and then, with luck I might be able to dilute some of the anger. Thus encouraged, in a state of total fatigue, I sought and found the blissful oblivion of sleep.

It turned out that the prelate took the high road and, realizing who was involved and what was at stake, deliberately played down the incident. His loathing of the Nazis—President Tiso the Catholic priest notwithstanding— earned him the admiration of the few remaining Jews in Zilina. Little did I know that his standing up against the Germans would eventually cost him dearly, and that I would be practically an eyewitness to the occasion.

In the orphanage, as I was getting ready to appear before the prelate, the incident seemed to emerge from a past so distant that he might not remember any of it. Too much had happened since that warm summer's day. And yet it was odd to think that finally I had to face him. No hiding in the bathroom this time. No way to elude *the test.*

I T   W A S   W I N T E R , and by the time we left the orphanage, darkness was already upon us. I was grateful for that. It was cold and clear; the new snow was half frozen and squeaked under our feet. Mother Superior and Sister C. must have found it difficult to walk in the snow, since they kept lifting their long habits with both hands. It was a beautiful movement, and one totally alien to the ways of nuns. Following a few steps behind, far enough to watch and yet close enough to feel a part of this strange group crossing the main square, I was aware of my anxiety building with each step.

Would the prelate remember me? Was he as good a person as my mother had described him to be? What would happen if I failed the test? And what would happen if I passed it? I could not understand what it was that they were after. Supposing that I was able to recall the long Latin prayers—what would it mean to them? Was it so strange? Was there something wrong with it? Perhaps it was blasphemy?

Suddenly Mother Superior slipped, and had she not caught Sister C.'s arm at the last moment, she would have fallen. A short sigh—an "aah"—was the only sound that escaped her lips. It was strange to hear Mother Superior saying "aah." I felt embarrassed trespassing on her privacy.

My stream of worries cut short by this incident, I could now concentrate on the task ahead. In my mind I went over the opening lines of several Litanies. I did not know their names—or even whether they had names—and the only way to recognize them was by listening to the opening lines. The problem was that many opening lines sounded similar, and it was only later in the Litany that their identity could be fully established.

The open space of the square was now behind us, and in the narrow street leading to our house there was hardly any snow. In this area protected from winds, the warmth of the tightly packed multitude of people produced a vapor that covered most of the shop windows. I had always liked the soothing transition of entering a warm shop on a cold day. How I wished now to enter one of the shops, which I knew were well lighted in spite of the taped windows. (To prevent detection by enemy—*enemy?*—aircraft, all windows were covered.) How I hoped that something would happen to prevent me from going to the prelate.

What if Mother Superior were actually to fall down and hurt herself? Would we still proceed, or would we call the whole thing off?

I knew that these were evil thoughts and that I must resist them. The Devil was trying again to plant himself in my mind, and I must be strong and good and chase him away. The only method I knew of was to say a few Our Fathers before it was too late. The priest who taught catechism in school was adamant about this. "Speed is important," he would tell the frightened class. "The Devil is quick to act, and if you give him just a few seconds in which to work, there is no way of knowing how it will all end." I never quite understood what exactly could happen, but somehow it suggested the terrible danger of "impure thoughts." There was certainly no shortage of impure thoughts in my mind. They would arrive suddenly out of nowhere, but most often they came in the evening, just before I fell asleep. Many such thoughts were pleasant, and were it not for the fact that they were terribly dangerous, I would have enjoyed thinking them for a long time. Lately, I had learned a good trick: I would prepare myself to fight the Devil with a devout prayer, Our Father at the ready, and, thus equipped, would allow myself to have a few impure thoughts, all the time knowing that help was close at hand. As the priest said, it was when we were unsuspecting that the Devil was most dangerous. By getting ready for him and then deliberately inviting him, the danger was much reduced. It worked most of the time.

The two sisters were moving very quickly, and, being distracted, I had a hard time keeping up with them. We were now at the end of the narrow alley, at the intersection with our street. It was here that the tall and beautifully decorated Christmas tree had stood a few weeks ago. Facing us were the stairs descending toward the lower section of the city, in the direction of the railway station. To our right was the main church, with its austere high walls. To the left, the second house on the left was where we used to live—where *they* now lived. The prelate's residence was almost directly across the street.

As we were about to cross, Mother Superior took me by the hand. Did she realize where we were? Did she sense what I was going through? Or was she perhaps worried that I might run away at the last moment? I did not care why she did it and was glad to hold her hand. Walking so close to her prevented me from turning around to take a quick look at the house. That was what I had planned to do prior to her intervention. As we entered the iron gate, just before ringing the bell, she gave me a close look, its warmth diluted by worry. Only much later did I realize that, in a way, she, too, was being tested; after all, I was her protégé, and it had been her idea to bring me here.

The doorbell was not an ordinary one; instead of buzzing, it made a two-note sound, like a real bell. It was answered immediately by an old woman whom I had not seen before. Either she was new or she had never come out of the house. Her back bent low, she barely looked at us as she took our coats and led the way to the prelate.

My heart was beating very fast. The way he stood up to welcome Mother Superior suggested a great deal of respect. He nodded his head several times and led her to a comfortable armchair. Next, he motioned to Sister C. to take her seat. Finally, he turned to me. I had not seen his

face very well before, primarily because his big hat always
cast a deep shadow. But now only a small cap, like those
of the Franciscan priests (very much like a Jewish
yarmulke), covered his graying hair. His dark eyes were in
marked contrast to his thick gray eyebrows. There was so
much light in the room that I could see the tufts of gray
hair growing out of both his ears. I didn't remember having
ever seen hair growing in ears and could hardly stop looking. His penetrating gaze did not allow me to pursue this,
however, and soon I found myself caught in the orbit of his
eyes.

For a brief moment, I thought I detected recognition,
but I could not be sure. There was a gentle hint of a smile
hovering on his lips. His was a reassuring face. I could now
take my place on a chair between the two sisters. The chair
was too high for me, and I could not reach it without
taking a helping hop, while at the same time holding it
with both hands behind my back. This accomplished, the
prelate returned to his own armchair, facing the semicircle
of visitors.

Now came something totally unexpected. The prelate
turned to face Mother Superior and proceeded to ask her
a long list of questions about the orphanage. They talked
about the food supply, the stock of potatoes and cabbage,
the harshness of this winter, and the difficulty of obtaining
enough coal for heating (it was pleasantly warm in the
room). Next he asked in detail about the plans for setting
up a field hospital for wounded soldiers in the orphanage:
where would it be located, and when could it start? It was
the first time I had heard anything about a field hospital,
and I felt proud for being able later to tell the others. That
issue exhausted, he now proceeded to inquire about the

well-being of all the sisters, most of whom he appeared to know quite well. It was obvious that he enjoyed Mother Superior's company, and since it was rare that they met, he decided to make the most of it.

My mind began to drift, and at one point my eyes met those of Sister C., who must also have been feeling ignored. I scanned the room for a crucifix but could not find one, unless it was on the wall behind my back. I felt a strong urge to check but did not dare to make the necessary movement. Finally, they started to discuss the state of the war, and I became all ears. Everything that was important to me hinged on the war and its outcome. The prelate spoke very softly, as if he were afraid of being overheard. He spoke of the Americans and the British fighting in France, and about how the winter slowed them down. Then he talked about the Russian front and the partisans, and at one point he said that the Germans were sure to lose. This last was practically whispered, but I heard it loud and clear. I would have heard it even if he had only thought it. Coming from him, it must be true. But when? How soon?

As if responding to my silent question, he warned Mother Superior that the Germans would not give up easily. They would fight until the very end, killing as many people as possible. And they would surely try to punish anyone who was suspected either of collaborating with the enemy or of just being happy to see them lose. This sounded exactly the way Apuka used to talk when he was explaining the state of the war in front of the huge map of Europe. Those who came to discuss this with him did not like to hear what he had to say; they rebelled against his chronic pessimism. How odd to hear the same things from the prelate himself.

He then proceeded to give Mother Superior some specific instructions that I could not understand. The words "field hospital" came up again and again, suggesting that it was a way to prepare for the final phase of the war. The Gestapo hated all religion, and the Christian leadership must prepare for the worst. Certain documents and precious items should be well hidden as a precaution.

I had the feeling that these matters should have been discussed privately, but for some reason the prelate had decided to throw all caution to the winds in order to get his point across. His words made a great impression on Mother Superior, whose frequent nods of agreement were becoming almost frantic: "Yes, Your Excellency"; "Of course, Your Excellency"; "Right away, Your Excellency." And so it went, on and on.

I could not follow their discussion anymore and, concentrating again on my own affairs, felt the beginning of what promised soon to become an urgent need to urinate. In the hectic moments of preparing for the visit I had forgotten all about it, and there was absolutely no way I could interrupt His Excellency with a request to use His bathroom. That would be preposterous, since in the orphanage the boys would never dream of using any but their own bathroom; nor would the girls, I am sure, use the sisters'. I wished I had relieved myself before coming to this place. Sitting on the high chair with my feet dangling in the air made it worse. I tried not to move, and then I tried not to think about it.

In the midst of my unsuccessful struggle I suddenly became aware that the discussion was coming to an end. The whispers and murmurs were replaced with a pause too long to be a part of what had gone before. It was only now, during the silence, that I realized it had been preceded by a meaningful change in the quality of the voices themselves and in the more formal version my name appearing twice, once from each side.

Sister C. changed her position in the chair, preparing for what was to come. All of them now looked at me, and Mother Superior said: "Juri, I have been telling His Excellency about your gift." (Why "gift"? From whom?) "He would very much like to find out more about it. You know that this is why we came here, don't you?"

"Yes, Sister."

"His Excellency would now like to ask you some questions."

"Yes, Sister."

The preliminaries out of the way, for the first time she leaned back deep into the cushions of the soft armchair. It was my turn now.

I was surrounded: in front of me was the prelate, who was free to treat me any way he liked, including finally settling his longstanding grievance over the embarrassing water incident. On my right was Mother Superior, who now seemed to be enjoying the role of detached spectator. Sister C. was on the left, between me and the door, barring any chance of escape. And, most important, behind my back was the crucifix. I had not seen it, but I could feel its presence in the tension of my neck.

[DURING MY LONG YEARS of university teaching, I have always been intrigued by the fright—indeed, the total panic—of most students taking oral examinations. As a researcher on stress, I could never find anything that even remotely approached the intensity of the anxiety involved. More than patients before major surgery, more even than soldiers before battle, young adults upon entering the examination room are often entirely lost. Their panic is unrelated to what is objectively at stake and largely unresponsive to prior experience. It is not the threatened outcome but rather the situation itself that is to blame. Being alone in a room with several examiners, at the mercy of their whims and their particular sense of justice, and having to prove oneself worthy probably evokes in many of us a host of prototypical parent-child situations, pregnant with emotional overtones. In my own case, sitting there on that fateful winter evening (for by now it was getting late), an orphan by all accounts, flanked by both the Good Mother and the Bad Mother, facing the Holy Father and with the Holy Son at my back, it was *the test* of all tests.]

"L O O K   A T   M E , my son!" said the father, signaling that the situation was being considered primarily from the religious angle. I met his eyes, trying hard not to look at the hair coming out of his ears.

"What is your name, my son?"

"Juri, Father."

"Juri what?" The ploy failed, and I braced myself for the inevitable.

"Juri Breznitz, Father."

A pause. The bushy eyebrows rose in concentration.

"Did you say Breznitz?"

"Yes, Father."

"Are you the son of Joseph Breznitz, who used to live across the street?"

"Yes, Father."

A dark shadow. Then the eyes softened.

"Were your parents taken by the Germans?" Making the water irrelevant, oh, so irrelevant.

"Yes, Father." Why only "Yes, Father"? Why not "Long ago, Father. Taken to Auschwitz, Father. I miss them, Father. I am afraid they were killed, Father. Will they ever come back, Father?"

He turned to Mother Superior. "Why did you not tell me?"

"I did not think it important, Father." Caught by surprise, instead of "Your Excellency" she used the currently available "Father."

"But it is, Sister, it is." This in a slow, detached voice. Then, back to me.

"When did you become a Christian?"

"Two years ago, Father."

"And are you a good Christian?"

"I hope so, Father."

"Do you say your prayers?"

"Yes, Father."

"Do you know your prayers by heart?"

So it was the indirect approach, like a fianchetto in the chess opening. The bishop (should be prelate) is developed sideways but sooner or later commands the long diagonal.

"I hope so, Father."

"Would you like to show me how well you know them?"

"Yes, Father." Finally there. If it were to take much longer, I would have to use the bathroom.

And so I took the test. He used the same book of Litanies as Mother Superior, and it went well. The Misereres went well, and the Liberas, and the Ora Pro Nobises, and when it was over there was a long silence. While searching my memory, I had looked down at my dangling feet, and even now I did not dare to lift my eyes. Exultant, and yet at the same time almost ashamed of this "gift" of mine, I recalled sitting on the high chair in the coffee-house, having just won a game of chess, waiting for Apuka (*my* father) to proudly pick me up and then, after putting me on the ground, but not before the slight delay of his embrace, take me by the hand and lead me out of the field of battle.

The prelate stood up, approached me, and gently stroked my head. I felt the softness of the hand and the hardness of the huge gold ring as it touched my forehead. He then prodded me (no picking up, no embrace) to get up from the chair and led me into an adjacent room. I was confused and forgot to check the crucifix behind my back. This new room was much darker, and there were pictures of saints everywhere.

"Wait here, my son."

He went back to the sisters, closing the door behind him. They were going to talk about me in my absence. The jury was in the next room deliberating my case. The urge to use the bathroom was now taking precedence over everything, but I was a prisoner in this room, and all the saints, including my own, Saint George, could not help me.

•   •   •

I T   W A S   O N L Y   much later, many months after the war
had ended, that I found out what was said after I had been
removed from the room. Today, I can appreciate how fortunate I was not to be present during that discussion. For
had I been there, the ability that had probably saved my
life would, transformed by knowledge, inevitably have
failed me.

At the same time, the reader, like the audience in the
dramatic theater, should know what happened. So here it
is, as told to me by my mother, as told to her by Mother
Superior:

It was winter again, although a very different one, and
we were sitting in the kitchen. I had just come back from
school, and on my plate were two large pieces of bread.
The bread was fresh and it was covered by a thick layer of
goose fat. Heaven itself. *"Durko moj"* ("My Durko," the
softest of the softest), "I must tell you something very
important," my mother said.

The hand reaching for the bread stopped halfway, and
so did my heart. There was only one topic that was
important, namely, news of my father. Had he come back?
Had someone seen him alive? Had someone seen him
die?

She must have guessed my thoughts, for, pulling her
chair closer, she said gently, "No, it is not about Apuka."
And then, "Go on, eat your bread, you must be very hungry." Savoring the fresh bread with goose fat, sitting in *our*
kitchen, with *my* mother close—it could not have been
more different from the previous event. And yet the con-

trast would pale in comparison with the strangeness of the story itself.

"Durko, do you remember the late prelate?"

My mouth full, I nodded my head yes. How could she have asked? Could it have been that everything that had happened before the earthquake seemed to her so unimportant as to be flushed from memory? Yes, I remembered him well. And I could not forget the way he probably died. I decided to tell her about it sometime soon.

"Do you remember having been to his house with Mother Superior?"

"Yes, and with Sister C. That was when he gave me the test." I must have been preparing for this, swallowing in time, mouth at the ready.

"This morning Mother Superior told me about it. You must listen carefully, for it is very important." A deep breath, and she was on her way. "The prelate was very impressed by what you were able to do. He said that never in his life had he come across anything like it. No person, and certainly not an eight-year-old child, could remember Latin prayers so well. He was sure that it must mean something important. Something that could not be explained by ordinary means [a miracle?] and was beyond normal human capability. Such an extraordinary memory must, in his mind, suggest divine intervention [a gift?] and should be seen as a *sign,* a promise of being singled out."

I took advantage of a short pause and evoked the lonely feeling in that room with all the saints, my feet crossed to control the need to urinate, while the jury was in closed session.

"But it was your being Jewish that the prelate found most exciting. He recalled the fable about a Jewish orphan who would one day become pope. He could not say where it came from, but it must have been quite prevalent, since the sisters recognized it. He urged them to observe you closely and to take very good care of you. With the end of the war approaching, it was particularly important to protect you from the Germans at all costs. It was essential to keep all of this secret; nobody, especially you, was to find out about it. And so, *Durko moj,* they did everything they could to save you, hoping all this time that as you rose in the world their efforts would pay off in the future."

I was speechless. Suddenly, certain things that I had not comprehended when they had happened made more sense. But the pope? Could it be that on the wings of a fable, the jury had been transported all the way to the Vatican?

"Fables go a long way in this part of the world, the good ones and the bad ones. [Jews using Christian blood to bake matzoth on Passover; Gypsies stealing children from their parents.] When the war was over, Mother Superior was so convinced that for a while she did not want to let you leave the orphanage. It was only after she realized that my coming back from Auschwitz did not fit the fable, since you were no longer an orphan, that she reluctantly changed her mind."

More incredulity. Be either an orphan or the pope. What a strange choice. Was Pope Pius XII an orphan, or did it apply to Jews only?

[JUDGMENT. The implications of all this for the sisters, and particularly for Mother Superior, are quite unfair. Was it only because of this strange fable that they saved me? Of course not. They saved Judith and they saved Rudo and Fisher, and there was nothing to suggest anything but genuine care about our safety. And yet, such is the price of awareness that the frightening thought, verging on the paranoiac, that they, too, were well protected for my sake would not go away. Recalling the desperate look on Sister C.'s face each time she attempted to hide me in the deepest and least accessible of the catacombs below the convent, I find it hard to reach a balanced verdict. But since on several occasions we were hidden before I took *the test,* this would indicate that, at best, it might have strengthened an existing commitment to human decency, without which nothing would have helped, anyway.]

Assault in the Snow

I call heaven and earth to
witness against you this
day. . . .

DEUTERONOMY 4:26

SEVERAL WEEKS had gone by since my test, and it
was now early March. Like the Germans, the winter would
not surrender, and the town was covered by a blanket of
fresh snow. It was also filled with new German units,
which were converging on the region from all sides. Some
looked old and battle weary, and some were fresh from the
Fatherland. These new soldiers seemed very young, perhaps no more than sixteen or seventeen. Lately, there had
also been many youngsters who belonged to the Hitler
Youth marching on the square. Some were German, and

some were Slovak members of the Hlinka Guards. In spite of my fear, I could not resist watching these parades. There was something powerful and exciting about the clean and shining uniforms, the coordinated beat of hundreds of drums, the swastika banners, and the dramatic sound of fanfares. I was scared and envious at the same time.

The Russian front was creeping closer to Zilina, and the sound of heavy cannons sometimes managed to travel the distance. On a clear night one could see the skies to the east turning orange. It was an awesome sight.

The nights were rapidly becoming noisier and more dangerous. Groups of drunken soldiers roamed the streets in search of suitable victims on which to vent their frustration. The famed discipline of the German army was deteriorating before our eyes. There were stories of rape and plunder, which the Kommandant vainly tried to attribute to the partisans. Twice a day, at noon and at six in the evening, right after our church bell struck the hour, the loudspeakers all over town would blare a phrase from Beethoven's Fifth Symphony. This had become a signal indicating that important news or messages would follow.

"Achtung! Achtung!" Always the hated German word before the announcement itself, which was in Slovak. (Through the power of repetition, the chilling opening words became for me an integral part of the beautiful melody, and have remained so to this day.) The news would tell of the German army's successes, particularly on the Russian front. Then there would be a long list of partisan atrocities committed against the peace-loving citizens of Slovakia, followed by an equally long list of actions taken against the partisans to protect the populace. The

more desperate the German situation became, the longer
these messages were.

Sometimes, the ancient system of messengers was also
used. The messenger would appear at an important intersection or in the main square and would commence drumming, until he was surrounded by those whose attention
he now commanded. Then he would put the drum aside,
unfold the declaration, and shout it at the top of his lungs.
This done, a copy of the declaration would be posted on a
wall or on one of the columns of the arcade. There was
something very dramatic about this archaic way of com-
municating, and it seemed well suited for Zilina, with its
medieval streets. The drumming itself was scary, and it
appeared that there were now altogether too many drums
around.

For as long as I could remember, the announcements
always meant something bad, and Mother used to freeze
whenever the loudspeakers went on. The only exception
had been during the ill-fated partisan uprising the previous
summer, but it had been very short. The few days of hope
had been quickly followed by a massive entry of German
soldiers and the Gestapo. For our family it had signaled
that all chances of surviving the war together were now
gone. The earthquake itself was not far behind. I wondered
whether the day would come when the loudspeakers
would play a different melody and carry different news.

It was Sunday morning, and after Mass several of us
went outside to play in the fresh snow. What we liked
most was to take advantage of the icy base for sliding. We
would run and then slide, often moving at great speed.
Fresh snow made it necessary for us first to work the

surface to establish a fully developed sliding path. This could be dangerous for innocent passersby, particularly if additional snow covered the slide. A single step on top of the hidden ice and a person would almost surely fall.

The square slowly filled with Sunday strollers, mostly parents with children. In spite of the snow there was no wind, and a weak sun was out. A chestnut vendor positioned himself at the corner across from the Grand Hotel. The smell was wonderful, but none of us had any money. We chose a spot toward the center of the square and started sliding. It promised to be a good long ride, one that would carry you on its wings for a full four or five seconds.

Suddenly, the distant sound of drums, getting closer. I tensed up, waiting. People started moving from the open part of the square to the darker, more protected areas under the columns. (All sides of the square had a colonnade, but most of the people used the side of the orphanage and the one next to it, connecting the Grand Hotel with the narrow alley leading toward the main church and the lower parts of the city. This odd preference for one side of a street or a square over another is a mystery defying all rational explanation.)

As the drums became louder, we, too, sought the safety of the columns, in front of the barbershop next to the orphanage. Then, slowly, we moved to the left, where the marchers might emerge at any moment. The drums ceased, replaced by the sound of many feet stepping in unison. The leaders of the Hitler Youth column could be seen entering the square. At their head were two banner bearers, the swastikas flying high. Next came the drummers, who I knew would shortly resume their beating. I had seen this choreography before. It consisted of drums signaling the approach from a distance, followed by a brief interlude of quiet to raise the tension, and, finally, as the main column reached the square, the drumbeats resuming to dramatize its arrival. What a wonderful feeling it must have been to march like that in silence, when suddenly the drums announced for everybody to hear: "Here I am! Take heed!"

There were no fanfares, but many of the marchers held black clubs, like the ones carried by the Slovak militia, in their right hands. This was something new. With the marchers' hands moving to the rhythm of the march, the clubs almost touched the snow at their feet.

"Why the clubs?" people asked softly. "Do they plan a pogrom? On whom? There are no more Jews left in this town. Not a single one."

As I listened, the familiar hollow feeling in my stomach reasserted itself. I imagined all these healthy and well-dressed youngsters combing the city for Jews. Clubs at the ready, they would desperately try to find a Jew—any Jew, even a Catholic Jew—in order to pursue their deadly game. Frustrated at finding none, their shouts would become increasingly violent: *"Juden! Juden!"* It was as if by their disappearance into oblivion the Jews were guilty of the greatest of all offenses. Unable to be killed twice, they had deprived the master race of its pleasures.

"Maybe they just want to scare us?" A new suggestion. "You know, so that we don't help the partisans."

"After executing so many people at random, why would clubs be of any use? This does not make any sense."

"They are running out of ideas."

"Maybe they think that youngsters are more frightening."

The drums took over, and it was impossible to hear anything else. The long line started marching around the square, moving clockwise. The leaders of the column were quickly approaching on our right, and yet there was no end in sight, as fresh troops keep coming. It was only when the snake made a full circle and its head came into contact with the long winding tail (no swallowing here, in mythical Ouroboros fashion) that the end could finally be seen. The head was now marching in place, allowing the tail to catch up and position itself. Then, on a single order, they all stood still. The square was very quiet.

Now came the *Sieg Heils*. Three of them. The leader shouted *"Sieg"* and they all responded with *"Heil!"* It must have been the same *Heil* that was usually attached to Hitler. This finale was followed by an order to stand at ease, and, with their feet apart, the marchers now held the clubs with both hands behind their backs. I searched for the leader (surely a taller youngster with a different, even more beautiful uniform) but was unable to find him. There had to have been one, or else they would not have been able to carry out these orders in such perfect unison. Unless—no, that would have been impossible—unless they had planned everything ahead, down to the smallest detail?

In spite of the snow, they wore only sweaters over their brown shirts, and no hats. They must have been very healthy to be able to march like that. Next they started singing one of the popular German war songs. It sounded like all the other such songs, and although I could not hear it clearly, the words *"Kamerad"* (comrade) and *"Krieg"* (war) and *"tot"* (dead) stood out. It seemed strange that they should sing a marching song while standing at ease. The rhythm invited movement.

That song over, they immediately started a new one, and then yet another, all similar, all describing the inevitable death in battle. With each new verse the voices grew louder, as if the singers were singing about their own death, or perhaps trying to fight it by shouting its name. Their faces red with exertion, their hands behind their backs clasping their weapons, their chests rising (not unlike when we were "sitting at attention" in Matejcik's class), their blond hair responding to the breeze, they were like one. Scared and fascinated, I watched the ritual.

Suddenly, the drums again: *trrrum, trrrum, trrrum, pum, pum.* And after a short pause, *trrrum, trrrum, trrrum, pum, pum.* The next pause was interrupted by shouts. The drums intervened again, smothering the shouting, but not for long. The shouting grew wilder, and the drums gave way; at first just some of them, with the rest quickly joining. Something was going wrong. They shouted in German, but I could not understand what they were saying. Then the voices became more coordinated, punctuated by the rhythmic movement of the clubs high above the marchers' heads. A few more shouts in unison, and, shocked, I began to understand.

"Jesus war ein Judenkind! Jesus war ein Judenkind!" Jesus was a Jewish child!

A tremor moved through the snake as it started to uncoil. Things were now happening very quickly. The head and the tail both pushed toward the narrow alley leading to the main church. The snake broke somewhere in the middle, and the mass of uniforms and clubs rushed in the same direction. Their progress slowed by the narrowness of the alley, frustrated, they pushed and shoved each other.

It took me a few seconds to come out of my stupor, but the excitement of the drama tempted me on. There was another exit from the square leading to the main church. It was slightly longer, but wider. Together with many others, I rushed to take it. Once the square was left behind the shouting could not be heard, and there was nothing to suggest the type of spectacle that we were being drawn to. We could well have passed for a crowd rushing to the football stadium or curious to see the wagons of a circus arrive in town.

The brown structure of the main church stood by itself, the fresh snow packed high against its massive walls. Out in the open we stopped in our tracks, seeking direction. Across the intersection the clubs and uniforms could be seen piling up. The crisp air easily carried the shouts to where we were standing.

"Jesus war ein Judenkind! Jesus war ein Judenkind!"

They kept on coming, the healthy and well-dressed Hitler Youth. Milling around the prelate's house, perhaps waiting for the rest to catch up, or perhaps just a little undecided, the snake was transformed into a mob. As more people kept arriving from the square, it was getting difficult to watch. Several of us climbed the wall surrounding the church. The snow on top of the wall was frozen, and my fingers hurt. When I finally managed to get up, it was just in time to see the door of the prelate's house breaking under the onslaught of boots and clubs. Several youngsters jumped into the opening. I thought of the ancient woman answering the bell and opening the door for us just a few weeks earlier.

The crowd gasped, watching the prelate in his Sunday robes being dragged out of his house and into the street. For a split second I caught a glimpse of his beautiful wide scarlet-banded hat, soon to disappear under the savage clubs. The shouts were getting louder still, as if those who were too far from the act found this the only way to participate.

And so it was that I witnessed the attack on the prelate from a safe distance. I never saw him again, nor did I dare ask about him. On that day I could not fail to see that some people were watching from the vantage point of the windows of our former house, right above center stage. Suddenly my eyes were flooded, and I started to run back to the orphanage. I felt close to this old and gentle man. He was a good person, and he was kind to me. In the quiet and solitude of our chapel, some of the simple words came: *"Requiescat in pace. Amen."* Rest in peace. Amen. And later, when the fear of violence finally took complete hold of me: *"A morte libera nos, Domine."* From death deliver us, O Lord.

Hiding

And a man shall be as a
hiding place from the
wind.

ISAIAH 32:2

THE FIELD HOSPITAL was now fully operational.
We had cleared an entire section of the cellar, removing
several barrels of sauerkraut, the dwindling heap of potatoes, and odd pieces of discarded furniture. After we had
thoroughly cleaned the place, the stretchers were brought
in. There were no sheets, but each bed had a blanket. The
blankets were very old, and our attempts to disinfect them
were to no avail. There were about forty stretchers in all,
neatly arranged in two rows. The smell of sauerkraut permeated everything. I liked it, particularly when a current of

air made it combine with the aroma of coal coming from the adjacent wing of the cellar. The thick stone walls were damp, and some were covered with moss. Two small lamps hanging from the high ceiling were the only sources of light.

The hospital in town had been totally overwhelmed by the constant stream of German soldiers arriving from the Russian front. By now there were not enough trains to take them back to Germany, and many lay on the floor in the long corridors. It was thus not surprising that the first patients started to arrive even before our field hospital officially opened.

"Hospital" was perhaps the wrong word for it, since there were no physicians, no operating rooms, and practically no medication. The sisters could act as nurses, providing water, a limited amount of food, some bandages, and an occasional aspirin. Patients who could not walk to the improvised latrine were given chamber pots, which the sisters dutifully emptied. Once every few days a patient would be helped to wash.

From the very beginning, it was clear that for most of the wounded, the main function of the hospital was to provide a place where they could be helped to die in the comfort offered by religion. The sisters would spend long hours praying with the dying, often calling on a priest to administer Extreme Unction.

THE FORTY BEDS filled quickly, and the wounded soldiers kept coming every day. Sometimes a truck would stop in front of the orphanage, unload several soldiers, and

leave even before the driver could see that they had been
taken to the hospital. I heard one of the sisters complaining
that this was done deliberately to make sure the soldiers
would be accepted. After all, no Christian would leave
wounded soldiers lying unattended at the entrance to one's
house. Those with lighter wounds often walked the entire
distance from the military front to town, arriving at the end
of their strength, too feeble to talk.

Although most of the patients were German soldiers,
there were others, too. As the front drew closer to Zilina,
the partisans became bolder, initiating many skirmishes.
One night when I was on duty, a wounded Slovak partisan
rang the bell and was admitted. His stretcher was put
around a corner, some distance from the others. Sister K.,
who was in charge, took me aside and made me promise
not to mention this to anyone, as the Germans might shoot
all of us. Soon there were others, and as the war situation
deteriorated for the Germans, the precautions became
gradually less elaborate.

Many sisters now devoted most of their time to the
hospital, and they needed all the help they could get. I was
becoming a very devout Catholic and would often volunteer for the night shift. It was an arduous task, and to skip
a night's sleep was difficult. That was exactly what I
wanted, and the harder it was, the happier I felt. The shift
consisted of a sister and a helper, usually one of the older
girls.

After the evening meal I would approach Sister C. and
ask about the night shift. On these occasions she would
scrutinize me, as if she was trying to understand something, and then she would promise to speak to Sister K.

about it. This quickly done—perhaps too quickly—she would come back with the permission. Once in a while Sister C. would not allow it, claiming that I must rest; but mostly she did not object.

Although in my vanity I had hoped that Mother Superior and Sister C. would notice my actions, I had no idea of their profound effect. They interpreted it as a sign of early holiness—yet another proof that the late prelate was right about me. Now that he had been killed by the barbarians, his words carried even greater weight. In the middle of the night, among the dying soldiers, the fable about the Jewish orphan who would become pope was taking root.

Meanwhile, the stench of gangrene was gradually gaining the upper hand over the sauerkraut. The wounds were full of pus, and there were not enough bandages, so the old ones had to be boiled and used over again. My German was improving, and I spent long hours talking to the soldiers. Sometimes I would lead them in prayer, and the German words of Our Father and Hail Mary began to sound familiar.

For some strange reason, most of the deaths took place during the night shift. At first I was scared of the sudden mask descending on a face, but then I started getting used to it. When the sister was not around, I would even have the courage to shut the glassy eyes. The gaping mouths were a different matter, and I often had nightmares about them. At times I thought that I could tell when somebody was going to die, but I was almost always wrong. My fascination with death became an obsession. Was that the main reason I volunteered for these nightly shifts?

I was supposed to hate all Germans, since they had taken away my grandparents, my uncles and aunts and cousins, and finally my parents. They had killed all the Jews, and if they were to find Judith and me, they would surely kill us as well. They even killed the prelate. But something was wrong; the Germans were supposed to be healthy and strong and victorious. The wounded soldiers in our field hospital were different. They were in great pain, they sighed a lot, and they spent a long time looking at pictures of their loved ones. And then they died. I could hate the SS and the Gestapo and Hitler and most Germans, including Hans, but not the ones who came to our hospital. And so I led them in prayer and gave them water and smelled their gangrene, without hating.

This evidence of compassion did not escape the attention of the two sisters who had been entrusted with watching my progress. Thus, when the need to hide me suddenly became evident, they were ready.

CONSIDER THE FASCINATION of hiding. Infants are sometimes tested for intelligence by being shown an object that is then slowly removed from their field of vision and put in a box or covered with a cloth. If the motion is not too abrupt, the infant can follow the object until the point when it is hidden. Out of sight, out of mind. His eyes return to meet those of the adult playing the trick. The object, even if it was a glittering and inviting one, has now ceased to exist. Only much later, when the infant has been freed from total dependence on the sensory here-and-now, will he be able to keep the object represented as an image in his mind long after its disappearance. Once that can be accomplished, the stage is set for the concept of looking for the unseen, of searching for that which is hidden.

The culture has yet to be found where children do not play hide-and-seek. Its universal appeal suggests that the rich experience it provides speaks to some important issues. First and foremost, it is a game of wits. The child who is hiding (the "prey") must anticipate where the seeker (the "hunter") will look for him. The obvious places must be avoided. The problem is that the hunter knows this, too. The children take turns playing both roles and are soon able to carry their knowledge from the one to the other.

Next there is the exquisite tension of the prey as the hunter is closing in: the need to be absolutely still, perhaps even to stop breathing; the anticipation of being discovered at any moment and yet perhaps to escape discovery. It can be intoxicating; it is the stuff that gambling is made of.

In one respect, important to my own story, the game can be misleading, since it almost invariably ends with the hunter succeeding in his quest. The lesson learned is that hiding at best only delays the final outcome. That was what my father used to argue each time someone would suggest going into hiding. Sooner or later the Germans would find everybody; their hunting of Jews was too systematic to be derailed by a temporary disappearance.

IT IS AN AFTERNOON, of course, and Sister C. enters, breathless. The Germans are already in the courtyard, and there is no time for anything complicated. She

urges all the boys to leave immediately, and I am quickly
pulled toward Hans's bed, in the middle of the room. She
covers me with the large down comforter, adjusts the bed
to hide my presence, and leaves. It is dark and I am having
trouble breathing. My heart beats fast, and I need a lot of
oxygen. The whole thing has happened too quickly, and I
am still disoriented. In her haste, Sister C. put me facing
the wrong way, and I can smell the pungent odor of dirty
feet.

A minute goes by, and just as I am becoming more
relaxed, the door to the right opens with the kick of a boot,
and the hunters enter. There are at least two of them,
maybe three. They shout something in German, but their
voices are muffled by the thick comforter. Then I hear a
female voice: Mother Superior? Sister C.? More German,
and then the sound of boots kicking the beds, and an
additional noise, such as may indicate the forceful removal
of blankets. I freeze. I want to take a deep breath and hold
it for as long as possible, but there is not enough air. The
smell is oppressive, and I start to sweat. As the kicks come
closer, I become preoccupied with absurd details: Why
Hans's bed? Because it is in the middle? Or because his
comforter is the largest? Or because he is German? And
then some bigger questions: Where is Rudo? And Judith?

It is obvious that they are coming closer and will soon
discover me. I am suddenly seized by an urge to remove
the comforter and inhale the fresh air. It is useless, anyway,
so why suffocate? Perhaps if I give myself up they will
show me some mercy. Certainly more than if they find me
hiding under the comforter. What a foolish thought; these
are Germans. It is like hiding from Death itself. Can one
hide from Death?

•   •   •

[I AM SURE that if I had been older at the time and
had known the Samarkand story, I would have thought
about it right then, under Hans's comforter. Once I had
heard it, it was forever at the ready to ensure that no
illusion would be allowed to dwell in my mind longer than
it took to recall the story's frightening simplicity:

A man is strolling in the marketplace when he is suddenly accosted by Death making threatening gestures toward him. He runs in panic to his master and asks his
advice. The master responds, "You must leave here immediately and go as far as Samarkand, so Death won't be able
to find you." Shortly after the man leaves, the master meets
Death on the street and complains about the threatening
gestures, to which Death replies, "I was not threatening. I
was only surprised to see him here, knowing that we have
a meeting scheduled for tomorrow in Samarkand."

Perhaps it was good that I did not know the Samarkand story; perhaps one should be forbidden to tell it
altogether.]

IT IS NOW the turn of the invisible sister to raise her
voice, and this leads to a heated exchange. However, the
noise of the boots stops momentarily. The shouting goes
on, but it appears to be moving toward the door. It settles
there for a while, hesitating to exit. I can't breathe, and my
head begins to turn. In a few seconds I will surely faint. I
decide to count to ten and then give myself up. The count
progresses, as if this were all just a game, and I slow down,
cheating. Then, slowly and methodically, the thought that

has been lurking in the shadows finally presents itself: "How did I sin to deserve this?"

Strange and complex is the fascination of hiding, for within it resides also the sense of guilt. We hide when we are afraid of punishment for something we have done. Did I not spend long hours hiding in the bathroom after the incident with the prelate? It is at this point that the hunter achieves his ultimate victory: his prey now believes that he deserves to be caught.

[FOR SOME REASON, the James-Lange theory of emotion focuses primarily on fear, suggesting that if I run, then I must be afraid. By the same token, it could be argued that if I am hiding, then I must be guilty.]

I AM NOW FACED with a new type of danger: the motivation of the guilty one to actively seek punishment. Now that I have tasted the gentle relief provided by confession and penance, the temptation to cleanse myself one last time is gaining strength. But what was my sin? Was it my Jewishness? Was it my arrogant persistence in staying alive when everybody else has perished long ago? Or perhaps my dreams of revenge against Hans? Was my good memory a sin? Was I trying to take advantage of this "gift" of mine in a sinful manner? And the night shifts—were they perhaps sinful attempts to cover for my inadequacy?

I am so preoccupied with these thoughts that it takes me some time to realize the hunters have left the room. I push aside the comforter to make an opening, a small beacon of light breaks the darkness, and my lungs fill with happiness.

My relief is short-lived, however. As I hear footsteps, I have barely enough time to pull the covers over me again before the door opens. Then Sister C. removes the comforter and whispers, "Quick, change into your hospital clothes and follow me. They went to fetch their dogs and will be returning soon."

No, not the dogs. Please, not the dogs. I jump out of bed, take from the communal dresser the dirty, smelly clothes I have been using on my night shifts, and start to undress. Sister C. is watching, and even now, while the hunters are prowling around the premises, I am worried about her seeing my circumcised penis. I change my shirt first, hoping that its long tail will be of some help. She urges me to hurry, and after some hesitation I remove my trousers and underwear, and change. She folds my discarded clothing and puts it in the dresser. We leave, she leading the way through the familiar alleys and stairs to the cellar, and then to the field hospital. Sister K. (does she know something?) takes me by the hand and leads me to the corner where the bandages are put on a Primus stove to boil. I look for Sister C. (we have come a long way together), but she is gone.

"Juri, make sure the water boils for a while before removing the bandages."

"Yes, Sister."

It had been a long time since I had last come to the hospital during the day, but it did not seem any different. Daylight could never penetrate here, anyway. The smell was somewhat weaker, though, and I wondered why. Even so, it was very powerful, and it permeated everything. My clothes carried it, too, and after a single night shift I could not wear them anywhere else. Matejcik would throw me out of class, and going to the chapel would be an intolerable intrusion on the wonderful smell of incense.

Suddenly I understood. I had been brought here to hide for more than one reason. The wounded German soldiers knew me and liked me, which might be useful. The place was familiar, and I could act naturally, unlike the hunted prey. But most important, the stench of gangrene would prevent the dogs from following my scent—any scent. This was the only place where their ferocious tenacity would be useless. The smell of death was the perfect camouflage for a "stinking Jew."

[H I D I N G   I N   T H E   O P E N is sometimes the best way to fool the hunter. For the gazelles of the African savannah, lost in the crowd, safety lies in numbers. But it can work only if the hunter does not care about the identity of his prey. When that happens, one's good fortune depends on the misfortunes of others. In humans, it is the perfect design for cultivating guilt. Among the few things concerning Auschwitz that my mother agreed to talk about was the daily selection of the thousands of bodies needed to feed the gas chambers. As one approached Mengele the hunter, it was important to walk erect, to have pinched the cheeks to look healthy, to inhale deeply in order to broaden the chest, and above all, not to look at him. And, yes, to hope that others in line would fail and the death quota would be satisfied for one more day.

From the moment the lioness or the cheetah singles out a particular gazelle as its target and commits itself in an open charge, the others do not matter anymore. It will pursue its prey relentlessly as long as it can, even if there are better opportunities around. For the prey, the realization that one has become a target sweeps away all other concerns. The Samarkand story is silent about this, but perhaps the man seeing Death roaming the marketplace tried to mingle with the crowd. For a while things might have seemed all right—until the moment when he was singled out, and marked forever.

"Why me?" asks the woman who has just been given the results of her biopsy. Once you are marked by cancer, that most efficient and silent hunter, nothing ever remains the same.]

I OBSERVE the boiling bandages. The bubbles pierce the densely packed cloth and on reaching the top are free to evaporate. New ones replace them, and the water is slowly changing color. Soon it will have to be replaced. When filled with water, the big cauldron is too heavy for one person to carry. After I remove the bandages, it will have to be carried first to the improvised latrine and then all the way to the tap and back. The fresh water is very cold, and it will take a long time for it to boil. Will the Germans find me by then? There is a mild excitement in watching the water for the first signs of boiling. But there is a lot to do before then, and a lot can happen.

If they are coming back with their dogs, that can only mean that they know whom they are looking for. As an extension of the hunter, the dog pursues a specific prey. Did someone tell the Germans about Judith and me? Was it Hans, with his smelly feet? Or did the Kommandant himself recall the secret that he had discovered on Christmas Eve? Perhaps he got some bad news from home? Perhaps he had drunk too much and talked too much? The possibilities are too numerous to count, and, comforted by the warm vapors and the steady hum of the boiling water, I slowly let go.

[LIKE AHAB'S QUEST for the white whale, the hunter's pursuit of his prey becomes an obsession. The thought that a few Jewish children were still loose somewhere in the vast sea of Europe was an affront to the master race, their elimination more important even than winning the war. Let the wounded German soldiers walk to the field hospital in Zilina; the trains are needed for shipments to Auschwitz. The hunter, like Ahab, oblivious to his own impending downfall, persists.]

"YES, OF COURSE they returned," said Sister C. in response to my question next morning. "What did you expect?"

"With dogs?"

"Yes, with dogs."

"And what happened?" I was worried about Judith. I knew that Rudo and Fisher were both all right, but at Mass I could not see Judith and had been afraid to ask. All the other boys had left for breakfast, and Sister C. and I were alone in the large room. Would she answer? Why assume that Sister C., or any sister, would conduct a dialogue with one of her youngest protégés? Fortunately, the temptation to tell the story was too powerful for her to resist.

"Mother Superior would not let them in. She stood in the doorway and would not budge. The leader of the group did not know what to do, and they went back for instructions. It did not take them long to return, with a higher officer leading the way. Mother Superior was still there, but he abruptly pushed her away. Imagine, the swine."

Excited, she stalled, and I worried that she had had enough of my questions. But I was wrong.

"All of the sisters wanted to block the door along with her, but Mother Superior wouldn't hear of it. It was too dangerous for the convent, she said. So we had to watch from the corridor."

"Where were the dogs?" A stupid, stupid question. It was the time I had spent in the hospital waiting for the dogs to arrive that had made me ask it.

"They were there, straining their leashes to get in. But Mother Superior stopped them."

"How?"

"I don't know, but when they started to push their way in, all three of them and the dogs, she shouted something, and they just stopped in their tracks and left."

They couldn't have been the Gestapo, then, since nothing would have stopped them. But what could she have said that made the hunter hesitate? And why? Why would she endanger herself and the entire convent for our sake?

·   ·   ·

[T H E F A S C I N A T I O N of hiding pales in comparison with the mystery of courage, particularly if one serves the other. It is when fear dictates *run* and the mind dictates *stay,* when the body dictates *don't* and the soul dictates *do,* that the heroic battle between courage and fear, its ever-present companion, is being waged.]

"B U T T H E Y W I L L be back, Juri. They will surely come again, and again, and again."

In March of 1945, the future still tilted toward the hunter.

The Bell

An horrid stillness first
invades the ear,
And in that silence we
the tempest fear.

JOHN DRYDEN,
"Astraea Redux"

IT WAS ON April 30 that I came as close to death as I ever have.

For several weeks, the front between the Germans and the Russians had been just a few kilometers from Zilina. We did not know that the war was practically over and that even Berlin had capitulated, but there was now no doubt about its ultimate outcome. For some reason, Zilina appeared to be among the last isolated islands of German resistance.

The sick and wounded who trickled to the improvised

hospital at the orphanage were now a mix of Germans, Russians, and partisans, all lying and dying one next to the other. For some time now the sisters had given up on any attempt to keep them separated.

The partisans were near, occupying the main mountain range above the city. There was intermittent shelling from the direction of Duben, the highest mountain to the north. Its contours could be seen from all points, and, once based there, the partisans could choose their targets at will. For several days and nights the shelling continued almost without cease. The sounds told the story. First there was the bass of the distant explosion, then a pause of a few seconds, followed by the whistling of the flying mortar, and finally the nearby explosion with its shattering noise. For the last few days we had all been living and sleeping in the cellar, not far from the place where the few remaining barrels of sauerkraut were arranged in a neat row. The field hospital was on the other side of the basement, but the oppressive smell of gangrene knew no limits.

Then, abruptly, the shelling stopped entirely. It was frightening to be confronted by this sudden silence, not knowing what it signified.

[I   O N C E   H A D a similar experience in East Africa. It was close to sunset, that most dangerous of all times, and we heard a leopard prowling nearby. All the animals and birds were hysterical, warning each other. This went on for some time, until with the growing darkness they must have realized that they had lost the leopard's exact location. Once that happened, they all hushed, practically at the same time. The tension of the eerie silence was further augmented by the knowledge of the near danger.]

THIS WAS NOW the third day without a single shot having been fired. It would be noon soon, and another day would go by without the bells ringing. The bells of our orphanage were an integral part of life in Zilina and could be heard three times a day, and more on Sundays and holidays. The belfry, overlooking the main square, was the tallest structure in town. There were two bells, of different sizes, and the heavier one was extremely difficult to ring. Its rope was very thick, and even by hanging on it without any support I could not make it budge. A much larger and stronger boy was needed to put it into motion. Once the bell had been started, however, it was relatively easy to maintain its swing. I always enjoyed the task of ringing the bells and would give anything to climb the long winding staircase above the chapel to help. There was something marvelous in the bells themselves, as well as in the powerful sound they produced. Hanging up there on the rope and feeling the strength of the bell lifting me up and then my own strength pulling it down—that was pure bliss. On several occasions I came up with one of the bigger boys, and while he rang the heavy bell I would take care of the smaller one. Its sound had a higher pitch, and it could swing much more rapidly, so I could ring twice for each of the heavy deep sounds. Playing such a duet, I would forget everything: who I was, where I was, and what was happening in the world. In some ways, the absence of their familiar reassuring sound during the last two days was even more frightening than the constant shelling.

Suddenly, for no apparent reason, Rudo and I decided to sneak out of the basement, climb the stairs leading to the belfry, and ring the bells at exactly twelve noon, as was the custom. After three days in the poorly lighted basement, the bright beautiful spring day came as a shock. As we climbed the stairs I was struck by the silence all around us. There was not a soul to be seen on the main square— something that I had not witnessed even during late-night hours. We struggled all the way up, arriving just one minute before noon. The clock was located just below the bells, and by leaning out we could touch it. For one whole minute we rested, breathing heavily.

Since both of us were skinny and could not hope to move the big bell alone, we decided to hang on to the rope together. As the time neared we grasped the thick rope and then pushed off from the last stair, hanging freely at the top of the belfry. Our combined weight had some effect, but it took more vigorous jumping before the bell struck. As soon as this happened, I let go and quickly moved over to the small one. A few seconds later, both bells were ringing merrily, as if nothing were the matter.

Then, suddenly, there was the whistle of a shell, and an immediate explosion, a heavy one, right at the center of the bell tower. Before we could realize what was happening, we were tossed aside by the explosion, luckily landing on the staircase. Everything was covered by dust, and we were in a state of shock. When the bells finally stopped ringing—why does it take so long for them to come to rest?—I discovered that I was bleeding. It turned out to be a superficial wound to a finger, but there was the clear mark of a piece of shrapnel. We waited for a while in apprehension and finally got the courage to go down the stairs and descend to the cellar. There were no more shots fired that day from Duben, nor from any other direction. As a matter of fact, this single shot, aimed as a response to the bells, was the last fired at Zilina, and although I know better, I would like to think it was the last in the entire European theater of operations.

[WHAT WAS THE MEANING of this shot, if any? Why the need to silence the bells? Was it a deliberate and rational decision on the part of some commander of the mountain batteries, or an irresistible impulse emanating from the depths of a battle-weary soul? Was the sudden sound of the bells carried to the peak of that mountain perceived as some type of defiance? Was it anticipated that the bells should remain silent until the moment we were officially liberated?

In one of his wonderful stories, Laurens Van Der Post describes the innermost subtleties of the character of a Japanese officer in command of a prisoner-of-war camp. He is the main source of terror for the inmates, and his capacity for hate and torture knows no limits. Then, one night, his behavior is altered under the influence of the full moon. Since, according to my mother, I, too, was once transformed by the full moon, I often think about the soldier who, like Othello, must have cried "Silence that dreadful bell!" and had to fire in the direction of its sound.]

·   ·   ·

T H E   N E X T   M O R N I N G   I woke at the usual time, although early Mass had been canceled, as it was too dangerous to leave the physical safety offered by the cellar for the spiritual one to be found in the chapel. The total silence that descended upon the city was simultaneously disturbing and promising, particularly since during the night we heard large convoys of military vehicles moving through. It could have been either the Germans leaving or the Russians arriving. The uncertainty made the long wait very difficult, and I felt the urge to look outside. There was no question of getting to the street, nor did I contemplate a repetition of the belfry experiment. I could only sneak upstairs to the second floor and peer out at the main square from behind one of the small windows.

Approaching the window, I saw that it was barely dawn. The main square was totally deserted. After the long night in the damp and stuffy cellar, I needed some fresh air, and I slowly opened the window partway. The coldness was invigorating, and I inhaled deeply.

Suddenly, there was a distant sound like that of a horse slowly trotting. Strange! What would a horse be doing in the midst of a battlefield so early in the morning? The sound grew louder; it appeared to be coming from the direction of the opposite entrance, on the right. I caught my breath, waiting. The empty colonnades echoed the sound, which now seemed to be arriving from all directions at once. I felt my heart beating fast against the windowpane, and my long-held hot breath, finally released, spread a thin film of mist on the cold glass.

Suddenly the sound stopped, as if it were hesitating. A few seconds later, I saw a lone rider in a green uniform

atop a white horse enter the square. It was like an apparition. He slowed down, made a half turn to the right, and
proceeded to circle the square. His head was erect and his
rifle hung against his back. It was a dignified and reckless
entry: nothing protected him from a lone sniper aiming
from any of the windows. And yet he rode his white horse
as if the entire town were securely his.

It was only when the rider was practically in front of
the orphanage that I recognized the Russian uniform. Having seen it in its bloodier form on some of the soldiers
seeking shelter in the hospital, I now witnessed it in its
most beautiful version. I wanted to shout: "The Red Army
is here! Liberated at last! The war is over!" But with the
apparition now so close, I was too scared to open my
mouth. Instead, I waited for him to complete the circle and
disappear into the dark alley before venturing back to report my discovery.

Too excited to properly describe what I had seen, I did
not make much sense, and none of the boys believed me.
Sister C., however, was sufficiently impressed to seek the
counsel of Mother Superior. For several long hours nothing happened, and everybody thought that I had taken the
story of the lone rider on the white horse from some children's book. All was quiet, just as it had been for the last
few days.

Then, around ten o'clock, all hell broke loose. Hundreds of tanks, cars, and armored troop carriers converged
on the city from several directions. It was the Red Army, all
right, and there was not a single German in sight. Thousands of people came out to greet the soldiers with flowers
and the traditional bread and salt. They, in turn, distrib-

uted sweets and chocolate rations to children, whom they lifted onto the huge tanks. By noon it was a carnival of music and dance and happiness. The Russian army had waited in order to time its entry for their greatest holiday, May Day.

I shall never forget the relief and the outpouring of joy visible on all the faces. Throughout that beautiful spring day I kept looking for the officer on the white horse but could not find him. Nor did I see any of the thousands of displaced persons who came in the wake of the liberating army. Their entry would start only on the following day.

Waiting

"Hope" is the thing with
feathers—
That perches in the
soul—
And sings the tune with-
out the words—
And never stops—at all—

EMILY DICKINSON

THERE WERE SEVERAL entrances to the city, and it was impossible to watch all of them. Most of the displaced persons came from the Russian front, and one could see the long lines moving along the muddy road. I spent many hours watching in silence. It was an endless procession of the weak and wounded, of all nationalities, traveling across the ruins of Europe. There was something hypnotizing about the slowness of the moving lines, suggesting enormous fatigue. The roads were damaged, and so were most of the bridges spanning the numerous rivers, making any advance an ordeal of endurance. There was very little to eat, and a great many of these odd travelers stood in line for the hot soup provided by the Red Cross. They toted bowls and plates of all types, which had now become highly valuable possessions. They carried very little else—perhaps an odd blanket or a pair of boots. Like our early ancestors who roamed the globe in search of subsistence, the witnesses of Auschwitz traveled light.

I eagerly searched among them for a sign of Apuka or Anyuka. It was difficult to look out for both of them, and for reasons that I did not understand, most of the time I found myself looking for my mother. Observing only women made my task much easier, but everybody was so thin, and many had their hair closely cropped, so that often I couldn't be sure whether the refugees were men or women.

Would I be able to recognize my parents? I tried to evoke their image, but without much success; I could not keep their faces in focus. Suddenly I became frightened that I would never be able to recall them properly, and that if they did not come back soon, their image would fade entirely. Trying harder did not help at all.

I discovered that the only way I could actually visualize them was to go over in my mind an entire episode in which they took part. For instance, I would recall a typical Sunday morning: Apuka would have arrived late the previous night, and, lying in bed, I could not be sure whether I had actually woken up and was hearing him and Anyuka talking in soft voices, or whether I was dreaming about what had happened a week ago. Upon awakening, however, I would know that he was at home in bed in the next room. Patiently I would wait for the signal inviting Judith and me to join them. We used to crawl in under the down cover and go over the last week in detail. By now Anyuka would have had time to tell Apuka about my latest mischief, and I knew that sooner or later I would be reprimanded. It was not easy for her to raise two children with their father absent, and when she was in despair she used to say, "Just wait until Apuka comes home—he will punish you properly!" However, if more than a few days went by, she would either forget all about it or describe it in a minor tone, and Apuka's ire would not be terribly serious. He could never become really angry on those wonderful Sunday mornings when the four of us shared the same big bed.

Years later, to save heating costs during the winter I would volunteer to warm that bed for Anyuka, shivering at first and gradually becoming more comfortable; and then, just as the warmth began to spread pleasantly through my body, I would call out that the bed was ready and quickly jump into my own cold one in the next room, shivering again.

Apuka was always on the right side of the bed, and on his night table were needles for his insulin injections. I knew he had to take them every day, but it was only after incessant begging that he finally agreed to demonstrate how he did it. Removing his pants, he showed me where the needles had left numerous dots on his thighs. He took some cotton, opened a bottle of alcohol (oh, the wonderful smell of that bottle!), chose a spot on his left thigh, rubbed it with the cotton, took an ampule of insulin, perforated it with the needle, drew the clear liquid into the syringe, measured the exact quantity, squirted the excess out, the insulin making a big arc in the air, and, before I could prepare for it, plunged the needle into his flesh. It was all very quick and matter-of-fact, and it is perhaps not surprising that I have never been afraid of injections and have always preferred them to taking pills.

So, in my search for my parents, I could start to run the film of such a Sunday morning, with the bed and the needles and everything, and for a while I could watch them playing their parts. But to fix them in a static portrait was impossible. It was always an unfolding episode, and, having a life of its own, it did not leave much room for observation. Sometimes I would try to stop the film for a while in order to see them better, but the picture would invariably fade, and the only way to get it back was to start all over again.

Why hadn't they given me their photo before they left? During these long months I desperately wanted a picture. It would have been so wonderful to look at them in the cold mornings; and on my way to school, just before coming to the dangerous crossings; and during school itself, when I could have put it between the pages of my notebook and peeked at it without Matejcik's knowing; and every time I felt hungry or miserable or lonely. I would have covered that picture with my kisses and my tears. It would have been the most precious thing—the only precious thing that I owned. But they chose otherwise, and there was no photo, and I was too young and too foolish to have thought about it at the time and asked for it.

Had they acted in the conviction that they would never come back and perhaps believed that having nothing tangible to remind me of them would make it easier to accept their loss? Was this a valid argument? Was it perhaps a valid argument on that day when, having secured our acceptance into the orphanage, they were mainly worried about making the parting easier? Easier on whom? In any event, it was an argument of only temporary convenience. After all, even the most painful of episodes retains its power only for a limited period and is necessarily blunted by time. And it is not just time per se but rather our attempts to overcome it that facilitate this emotional leveling. How odd that by reliving the same drama over and over in our minds we inevitably introduce into it a measure of gradual composure. How odd and unfair, considering that those unique events are supposed to retain their emotional flavor forever, sustaining us in our times of everyday-life dread.

Did my parents take pictures of me and my sister with them? And, if so, would they recognize us? When I had last seen my sister I had been struck by how much she had changed. She was much taller, and in spite of her being so skinny, I could see her newly developed breasts. And what about me? Had I changed? I felt so different, but did it show? I found it almost impossible to consider myself a direct continuation of the clean and well-educated boy from the good family that I used to be. In the first place, I had broken my glasses in a fight and they had never been replaced. My closely cropped head was covered with sores from a skin disease shared by all the boys in the orphanage. I was thin to the bone, undernourished, my eyes were always red from inflammation and an occasional sty, and my nose was usually running. I had no handkerchiefs left, and I had learned to improvise with the fingers of my right hand. And yet I was still me, and when they came they would surely recognize me.

But what if they never came back? What a sinful thought! It is a sin not to trust in God, and it is a sin to lose hope. I clearly remembered that the priest had said so during Mass. Like all temptation, the sinful thought lurks in the background, waiting for the opportunity to present itself when it is least suspected. The surprise makes it very difficult to defend against, and before being cast away it leaves a mark, an indentation on the soul. This must be the work of the Devil himself, and, devout Catholic that I am, I quickly cross myself. And yet it does not always work, and the possibility that my parents will *never* come back makes some inroads into my consciousness, as if preparing the ground for a more potent return next time.

The word "never" is a frightening one. It is most often used when describing the suffering in hell. There the sinners will stay forever, *never* to be given another chance. How long was never? With Anyuka, even the longest of punishments was over in a few days. Was never much longer than that? After Jozo had given me a particularly nasty beating, I made up my mind never to forgive him. However, that was some time ago, and I cannot even remember the reason for our fight, or if there was a reason. When one is a child, never is either just a short time removed or else utterly incomprehensible. When the thought of my parents never coming back crossed my mind, it started out as the first but, once addressed more closely, quickly turned into the second.

Days went by, and the stream of people passing through our town did not diminish. Those arriving now must have come from distant places, perhaps from Poland or Germany, or even Russia. Once in a while I saw a horse pulling a cart filled with people. The horses had also had a difficult time during the war, and many were killed for meat. In Zilina there was a paper mill that was transformed into a sausage factory. The sausages were made of wood fiber mixed with horse meat. I ate it once, and it was very red and sweet. Although I was hungry, when I was told of its source I felt nauseated and could not finish my small piece. The horses pulling the carts were lucky to be alive. They looked old and tired, particularly when trudging up-hill toward the center of town. Our orphanage was at the highest point this side of the river Vah. Some of the horses were forced to go all the way up, only to have to go down the other side. I felt sorry for them, and whenever I heard their hoofbeats on the cobblestones of the square I had a strong urge to go down and watch them from up close.

These days we had more free time than before, as if the end of the war had released the rigid routine of our life. I can't say what it was that had actually changed, but things felt different. We still got up at five-thirty and attended Mass and had our bowl of caraway soup and went to school and did our duties as we always had, and yet things felt more relaxed. Could it be the spring, which had brought a great relief after this coldest of winters? Or was it perhaps the sudden change in Hans's appearance? He looked smaller and less sure of himself now that the Germans had lost the war. I was no longer a constant target for his whims, and at times I thought I saw a sad plea in the way he looked at me when nobody was watching. Was he sorry, or was he afraid? Afraid of the Russians and the partisans, who were combing the town for collaborators, or afraid of God's punishment in hell? Could it be—no, that was impossible, and yet—could it be that he was just a little afraid of me?

Now that some of my prayers had been answered, did it mean that the rest would also come true and things would be better soon? Or maybe just the opposite? After defeating the Germans, might God, in an attempt to be evenhanded, kill my parents? Or perhaps it was the other way around: After the Germans killed my parents, did He make them lose the war? If any of this had happened, I would be waiting in vain.

When the frightening effect of such thoughts became too much for me, I often reminded myself (how strange, that of all things it should be this) of the promise the German Kommandant of Zilina had made to Judith on Christmas Eve: "Don't be scared, your mother and father will come back." He was a very important German officer, and he could have known something when he said this so confidently. Besides, he was the only one who had made such an explicit promise, which increased its value. I don't recall that Apuka and Anyuka had promised to return, although they could have. Why not make such a promise to two little children who still take promises very seriously? Was it for the same reason that they had not left a photo? Did they, too, know something that they could not share with us?

HOW STRANGE IS the act of waiting. It is an attempt to fill time by jumping over it, by introducing the future into the present. This so purely human of all activities tries to tempt, nay, to force events into the mold of one's wishes and hopes. And then there is the preoccupation with time, the object as well as the vehicle of waiting. The problem is that the very effort to fill it makes it expand, and by focusing on it, we stop it in its tracks.

The tension of waiting is greatest when the imminence of the anticipated event is known ahead of time. As it gets closer, the emotion associated with it monopolizes our entire being. In contrast, when one doesn't know when the anticipated event will actually take place, it is impossible to maintain the tension for a long time. After a while, even waiting for something important can become routine. And yet whenever there are signs suggesting that the event is getting closer, the excitement immediately mounts.

Often we wait for small things, and once in a while for big things. The way we are, the small things may easily assume the importance of big things. "Small waiting" is not much different from "big waiting."

In some ways, waiting is the ultimate in passivity, the embodiment of helplessness. That may account for the fact that under its unfriendly aegis even the smallest, obviously unwarranted threat may acquire the power to dominate the mind. Here is a simple illustration:

Think of waiting for someone dear to you who is late for your meeting. There is no way to get in touch with him or her to find out what has happened, and the only thing left to do is to wait and hope for the best. And, in fact, optimistic thoughts are clearly the dominant ones, at least for a while: "He/she will surely come soon. It is only ten minutes past the appointed hour, and there is no reason to worry." You may even return to reading your book, only to discover that your mind is wandering and that although you are going through the motions of reading, you are not taking anything in. Sitting suddenly becomes uncomfortable, and you stand up, moving restlessly from one place to another. You turn on the television and flip through the channels, never watching long enough to be absorbed by what is offered. Everything seems irrelevant and unimportant, and before long you are checking your watch again. It is only twenty past the hour, although it seems like much longer since you last looked. "He/she must have missed the bus, or the train, or the traffic must be very bad," you think, trying to take charge of what now feels like the beginning of an unpleasant situation.

As more time goes by, you realize that such reassuring thoughts tend to work best the first time they enter your mind. Evoking them on subsequent occasions is gradually less effective, as if with each use they lose some of their credibility. You try to set your mind at rest by recalling that this is not the first time this has happened, and on all prior occasions things eventually turned out fine. This makes you—for the first but not the last time this evening—angry at the person who is late. Oddly enough, there is something comforting in being angry, since it implies that the person is all right and the issue is one of inconsequential and yet irritating neglect.

At some point the strange and frightening thought that something might have happened to prevent him or her from coming manages to enter your consciousness. A fleeting worry about an accident, with the accompanying visual images, is a possible scenario. Statistics notwithstanding, such ideas do cross your mind, even if only for a short while. The more extreme the thoughts, the easier you find it to dismiss them by resorting to logic and common sense. And yet, even when they are peremptorily dismissed, they leave something behind, an aftertaste of a devastating possibility. Perhaps the most important effect of such a brief consideration of a disaster is that it paves the way for similar thoughts in the immediate future. Thus, as the waiting stretches out, you become gradually more exposed to such disturbing possibilities.

To shake them off you go to the window and look outside in the hope of actually seeing the person coming. After a while you decide not to look, as if by looking you are keeping him or her away. Next you decide to count to one hundred, hoping that by the time you reach the end of the count he or she will be there. Halfway through you slow down, cheating. Nothing seems to be working anymore, and it is at this point that you first think that the person might have forgotten about the meeting. This is too painful to dwell upon seriously, perhaps more painful even than the thought of an accident. And yet there is an even more devastating possibility, which slowly drills its way into your consciousness: "Perhaps he/she did not forget, but does not wish to come."

You have now reached the bottom, since there is nothing more difficult than to consider the possibility of loss of love. The implications are too harsh to consider. They touch the most vulnerable part of the soul. Your anxiety threatens to overwhelm you. You pray for the person to come. Just this time, *please!* You ask yourself if you are guilty of doing something wrong that might have caused this. You promise to make things better in the future, you even promise not to be angry—a commitment easily forgotten once the door opens and the waiting is over.

Thus, waiting is particularly effective in quickly peeling off the superficial shield that provides our false sense of security and composure. We are never too old to overcome the child in us, afraid to be abandoned. But I was a child, and I was very much afraid. And so, day after day I roamed the various entrances to the town waiting for my parents' return. It was a "big waiting," the biggest of my life.

H O P E   P R O V I D E D the fuel that fed the images of blissful reunions. There were many such imagined reunions, occurring at different locations and having different flavors. The most common was of the classic type: I am standing alone in front of the orphanage looking across the wide space of the central square. Two figures enter the square from the other side, the one leading to our house. I feel enormous tension and with great effort stay put. Halfway across the square I finally recognize them, and all three of us start running toward each other, at first hesitantly, then in growing impatience, ending in an embrace of total abandonment.

Yet another image was that of myself walking past our house and suddenly seeing lights in the windows on the second floor. "They are back!" I realize, but I cannot be sure, and for a long time I spy on the windows. "It can't be them; they would have come to look for us immediately," I tell myself, and yet I am not sure and, spellbound, hang around the house hunting for a clue. At some point I see a shadow approaching the window—just a shadow, but it looks very familiar. After more hesitation I open the front door, climb the stairs, and ring the bell. After what feels like an eternity, the door opens and it is them, oddly looking well, not at all like the others coming back from the concentration camps. They embrace me, but in the midst of my uncontrollable crying the thought crosses my mind that perhaps they have been living here all this time, that they had not been taken by the Germans after all.

The image I liked most was that of my parents coming during the night, approaching my bed on tiptoe, and gently kissing me on the forehead. I wake up, and, sleepy and uncomprehending, put my arms first around one and then around the other, and with a happy smile take up my things and, as on the earlier occasion when we had left the camp, leave the orphanage forever.

FOR MANY MONTHS, I had done my best not to think about my parents at all, afraid of where my thoughts might take me. However, now that the war was over, it became a constant preoccupation.

I wished I could control these images, but often they would come and go on their own, in spite of myself. Sometimes I would play one of them out under the strangest circumstances. Once they entered my consciousness, it was very difficult to remove them without playing them out until their usual end.

I often tried to think about our reunion the way I imagined my parents must have been thinking about it. Walking with the rest of the displaced persons from one town to another, slowly approaching Zilina, they must have wondered whether Judith and I were still alive. Perhaps they had heard rumors about our death? Perhaps they knew what had happened in the other orphanage when the Germans came? Perhaps they were coming only in order to verify what they had suspected all along? Since I knew that both Judith and I were alive, there was a particular pleasure in thinking about it this way. By juxtaposition it assumed that they, too, were alive. I thought that it must be easier walking toward Zilina than passively waiting here for their arrival.

If they were late in coming, did it mean that they were dead? Were the distances sufficiently long and the roads sufficiently bad to allow for the possibility that they were still alive? Could they have forgotten all about us? In the hospital where I worked I saw many soldiers with head injuries who did not recall a thing, not even their own names. They seemed to recognize me and Sister K. but recalled nothing from their past.

And if my parents were alive, and did remember, and the distances were not so great, and the roads not so bad, did it mean that they did not want to come back? I had done a lot of mischief and had often disobeyed, but did I deserve such a punishment? And what about Judith? She was good and much loved by both of them, so it didn't make sense.

When the torture of waiting was finally lifted, it was, of course, unlike anything I had been rehearsing.

Eyes

Whence are we and why
are we? Of what scene
the actors or spectators?

PERCY BYSSHE
SHELLEY,
"Adonais"

HER NAME WAS MARINA, she was about Judith's age, and she lived in a small house opposite our own. The house was painted light blue, which was rather unusual for this part of the world. Several steps led up to the entrance, and Marina liked to sit there watching the goings-on in the street. Our street was called Dolny Val, which in Slovak means lower fortification, and dated back to medieval times, when the central core of Zilina was protected by several concentric circles of walls and trenches. Oddly, though, I don't remember any upper fortification, although

the name clearly implied this. Sometimes I saw her from
our window or from the balcony. On one occasion she was
sitting on the steps talking to a friend and I managed to
position myself so as to be able to steal a glance between
her knees. It was very exciting, although I felt hopelessly
awkward pretending to have lost something on the pavement. Marina must have realized what was going on, and
yet she did not close her legs or otherwise give me away.
I had not seen her since the day I had entered the orphanage, although for a short while I used to think about her
before falling asleep. That, however, had been a long time
ago, and when she suddenly appeared in the courtyard
looking for Judith and me I was very confused. She looked
much taller than I had remembered her, and despite her
thinness, I could see the beginnings of a well-rounded
figure. The ruddy cheeks and high cheekbones were still
there, and so was her broad smile, which appeared to be a
permanent feature of her face.

   But on this occasion my excitement was of an entirely
different kind, for immediately upon seeing her I knew
that something important was about to happen. After all,
why else would she come looking for us all of a sudden?
Judith, pale and obviously distraught, pressed her for information.

   "What happened? Quick, tell us what happened!"

   Marina, however, stood her ground, and besides urging us to follow her, she obstinately refused to say another
word.

   "But please, *please* just tell us if they are alive!"

   I thought Judith would burst into tears any moment
now, but she did not. After some more useless pleading,

she took me by the hand and the three of us started off in the direction of our street.

A N D   W H E R E   W A S I all this time, when this part of my life was enacted around me? The difficulty of the answer is commensurate with the strangeness of the question. After all, where could I have been? Why ask?

First and foremost, by virtue of being one of the dramatis personae, as the story accelerates I find myself center stage, blinded by the strong lights of its emotional impact. As on that earlier occasion, when walking the same short distance between our home and the orphanage in the opposite direction, the anticipation sends waves of trembling through my body. I can hardly breathe, and my heart races. As we rush under the archway, Judith presses my hand and half asks, half answers, the unspoken question that is in both our minds: "It's Father?" And I, almost immediately, without any hesitation, respond, "It's Mother!" How strange; both of us use the Slovak words rather than the "Apuka" and "Anyuka" of Hungarian origin, as was our habit at home. It is as though we realize that something fundamental has changed, and there is no way of returning to what our family used to be before it was torn apart.

T H E   D E T A I L S of that short walk that may yet turn out to be the bridge between darkness and light are so vivid in my memory that in addition to being at the center of the drama, I must, at the same time, have observed it from afar. It is as if the mind, the organ of awareness, while at the very core of everything, is, like the eye of even the mightiest hurricane, an area of paradoxical tranquillity.

I remember the light of the open square and the shadows of the colonnade, the feeling of Judith's hand in mine—she is on my right—and Marina's fast trot slightly ahead of us, her urgency more telling than anything she could possibly say. And yet, the details of the promise signified by her impatience are so important now. I have to know whom she is guiding us toward: Is it Father, as Judith believes, or Mother, whose image I now vainly try to invoke for the thousandth time? The questions are many: Why only one of them? Why hasn't she come straight to the orphanage? Is she sick? And why has Marina, of all people, been sent to fetch us? And why is it taking so long to cross the tiny square?

For some reason I cannot understand, we do not run, and our walk, although quite fast, is actually well measured. The reason cannot have anything to do with wishing to display the dignity of composure; we are much too young for that. The anxiety of facing what we both yearn for and worry about is probably a more accurate explanation. Or perhaps it is an attempt to approximate that earlier traumatic walk as closely as possible, as if such a corrective experience would undo part of its damage. Whatever the reason, Marina, who is not aware of any of this and yet knows something that we are not privy to, keeps skipping ahead, then stopping to wait for us and urging us to be quick. At some point the frightening thought occurs to me that Mother might be critically ill and speed of major importance. Fortunately, Marina's steady grin suggests otherwise.

The square finally behind us, we enter the dark, narrow alley that connects it directly with our street. In the past I have used it hundreds of times, but since entering the orphanage I have tried to avoid it; the proximity of the all-too-familiar surroundings was too upsetting. Context, after all, is everything. And yet I know the strange feeling of intimacy, verging on the claustrophobic, produced by the transition from the open square to the medieval atmosphere of this street. On some days, particularly during the early evening hours, one can barely squeeze through the multitude of people throbbing within this bottleneck. When running away from someone, either in play or in earnest, I would sometimes seek the protection provided by its human density. Once I was there, the fact that most boys could run much faster than me lost its significance, and my tiny physique actually became an advantage. Mother sometimes used to shop there, for both sides of the alley were packed with small shops of all kinds. As one approaches the end, there is a distinct sense of relief of pressure, and at the exit one is rewarded with a magnificent view of both the mountains and the lower section of the town. It was there that the municipality would put the Christmas tree each year, and it was there that we lived, right across from the by-now-violated prelate's residence.

Once out in the open, we make a sharp left turn in the direction of our house, but Marina shakes her head and pulls us toward her own house, to the left of the prelate's. There is too much light, and it is too hot; I can feel the perspiration where Judith's and my hands touch. The stairs (the famous stairs) leading to the entrance are narrow, but I don't let go of Judith, and she practically drags me up. I catch the sound of whispering coming from the room to

the right, and as we approach, it suddenly stops. Several
people, apparently Marina's parents, come out of the room
and either disappear or else stand in the doorway to watch
the unfolding human drama. I cannot tell which, because
once I have been gently pushed into the room, the vantage
point of an observer is lost to me entirely, to be reinstated
only much later, after the storm. Thus, I am left with the
narrow focus of the principal actor who, on top of everything else, is suddenly struck by stage fright.

In the room the blinds are drawn, and it is almost
totally dark, but I can make out the silhouette of someone
sitting on a sofa in the corner. Whoever it is can see us
entering, because I note something stirring in the shadows.
The short, involuntary movement comes at the same time
that I hear myself taking a deep breath, the action sound-
ing like a long whine, followed by a sense of extreme
pressure in my chest. I have now stopped breathing entirely.

Gradually, my eyes adapt to the darkness, and the
contours of a thin face, surrounded by cropped hair not
unlike my own, begin to stand out against the background
of the large pillows on the sofa. It is a sick face, a haunted
face, like the nameless visages I have been watching pass
through the town. There is something all those faces share
that makes them appear similar. And yet, this one looks
oddly familiar. I can't be sure yet, but the more I look—
and by now I am spellbound, unable to resist the mag-
net—the stronger the feeling of impending recognition.

It is at this point that I actually recognize the eyes,
which although deeply sunken into their large sockets are
now looking at me, and their unmistakable warmth removes the last of my doubts.

"Mother!" I cry, finally letting the air escape the prison of my lungs. "Mother! Mother! Mother!"

Once the spoken word breaks the spell, there is nothing to hold me back. Letting go of Judith's hand, I hurl myself in the direction of those eyes, and Mother, opening her arms to embrace us both, utters the first muffled sob, which quickly gains strength and, joined by those of the rest of the trio, mounts in a crescendo of uncontrollable weeping.

GENTLY NOW. Let nothing, not even the softest of words, touch that moment. For a while—at least a short while—it ought to rule supreme.

WHY DO HUMANS cry out of happiness? Is it direct testimony to its frailty? There is, after all, a close affinity between happiness and sorrow, since the smallest detail in the way chance plays out our life may transform the one into the other.

It was chance that struck the heaviest blow to my parents' ability to maintain hope of our survival. Mother told us the story shortly after the first attempts to displace the tears with laughter began to assert themselves. It had happened in Auschwitz. After Mother and Father were removed from the train, just before they were separated, they suddenly saw a group of children and were shocked (still capable of being shocked?) to recognize among them all the Jewish converts taken in by the Benedictine orphanage. It had been only two days earlier that they had seen the children in the security of the convent, paraded before their eyes to show why there was no room for Judith and me. The Benedictine orphanage had been my parents' first choice, and had they been successful in getting us in, we would have met briefly in Auschwitz, just before being sent with the rest of the children to the gas chambers.

But that incredible stroke of luck was marred by a more threatening question: How did it happen that the children were taken by the Germans? Either the Benedictine sisters had given them up, or else the Gestapo knew that there were Jewish children in hiding. In either case, the chances that the two of us were still safe appeared minimal. We might actually have been in Auschwitz already. My parents started searching for us, desperately wishing to fail. (How does one look for something that must not be found?)

"I wonder why I had to see those children. After all, nothing but despair came of it. And yet, in spite of everything, it was only the hope that you were still alive that pulled me through."

This was followed by a long round of hugs and kisses to reassure ourselves that this was not just another fantasy.

"We were afraid that you would never come back," said Judith.

"You were so late in returning."

Mother stroked her head and replied softly, "I could not come earlier. I was too weak to walk." And, after a short while: "And I did not want you to see the way I looked. Even now it must be frightening to see me like this."

Always the lady. Always dignified. The darkness now made sense. So that was why she had not come to the orphanage. Asking for the shutters to be closed, and positioning herself in the shadow in such a way that her essence would be recognized before we could attend to her external features—everything now made sense.

[WHEN MOTHER DIED, with the exception of a few photographs I did not care to keep any of her material possessions. However, there is one small item that Judith and I cherish above everything else. It is the dirty and broken comb that she brought back from Auschwitz. She traded it for a full day's ration of bread in order to have a chance to comb her closely cropped head.]

"HAVE YOU HEARD anything about Father?" (How odd. She, too, used the Slovak "Otecko" rather than the Hungarian "Apuka." So it is a new beginning on all sides.)

"No," we say, "nothing. Have you?"

"Not yet, but we must be patient."

And she proceeded to tell us the story of our father's return from the Russian POW camp after World War I. It sounded familiar, but in the present context it made new sense. He had been an officer of the Austro-Hungarian hussars and had fallen into the hands of the Russian army prior to its disintegration. When the war ended there was no word from him, and after a while his family took him for dead. It was only two years (*two years*) later that he suddenly arrived from Siberia.

I wondered about the implications of this story: Would we have to wait so long? Did it indicate that our father, having come back against all odds once, would surely return this time as well? But even in my wildest dreams I could not anticipate that this story of hope would keep my mother waiting for him indefinitely—against all information to the contrary, in spite of the diabetes that required a daily injection of insulin (in Auschwitz?), waiting not for one year, not for two years, but forever.

Memory Fields Revisited

Sweet is the remembrance
of troubles when you are
in safety.

EURIPIDES,
Andromeda

I HAD BEEN putting off my visit to the old places for
years. The arguments were a mixture of prudence and lack
of interest. After all, I used to say, there was nobody left
alive, and places as such did not interest me. But with the
collapse of the old regime, safety was no longer an issue,
and I realized that my professed indifference was at best a
poor excuse. Thus, it was not surprising that when I finally
decided to make the journey, I "cheated" right and left.

First, the entry was planned through Prague, the beautiful "Prague of a hundred spires," where I had never been

before. A different part of the country, a similar and yet different language, and the inviting sights of the city ensured that, at least in part, I would be an observer, almost a tourist.

Furthermore, during the first part of the trip I was scheduled to engage in some professional activities with Czech colleagues. My role as an academic discussing scientific issues was a well-rehearsed one, carried out under the safe aegis of objective detachment. It was also a latecomer to the wide gallery of different selves that combine to produce a person. It was acquired elsewhere, many years after the earthquake.

Most important, however, was the fact that I was not alone. My wife, Zvia, was with me throughout the journey. She served as a bridge to a present so different that any impact of renewed contact with the past was necessarily blunted. Thus equipped, I took the trip. My choice of winter was deliberate, and it was not cheating. Most of my memories are associated with the cold.

THE FLIGHT FROM Tel-Aviv to Prague was on Swissair via Zurich. The comfort of neutrality delaying the impact was suddenly shattered by the pilot's announcement that our path was over Nuremberg, of all places. I closed my eyes and visualized the splendor of the pagan ceremonies that took place there half a century ago. My imagination was a prisoner of films and pictures that I had seen over the years. They were simple and banal. After a while, with eyes wide open, I preferred to watch the monotony of the thick layer of clouds that appeared to cover all of central Europe. My eyes could not penetrate their protective cordon, and the earth underneath was unreal. During the stopover at the Zurich airport I had too much wine for lunch (more cheating), and now wished I hadn't. The small, insignificant fears of what lay in store passed through my mind in slow motion.

Would I be able to understand the language? Would the winter be harsh? Was it wise to rent a car? Did they have adequate snow-clearing equipment? Would they stop me at the border? Was I still persona non grata? Was my passport, which stated my birthplace as Bratislava, suspicious? And the visa, was it in order?

I knew that these were foolish concerns. After all, thousands had been here before me. Even Judith had visited twice already, coming back with stories of the orphanage, which had been turned into a museum. The chapel was still there, but everything else was unrecognizable. Since 1950, priests and nuns had been treated as enemies of the state. With few exceptions the priests had had to give up the public practice of religion, and so had the nuns. They had had to leave the hospitals and the schools and work in the fields and in heavy industry. For forty years they were dispersed all over the country, in small groups, trying to maintain some semblance of their vocation. Was there a chance that some of them were still alive?

A T L A S T ! Inexorably, like a person obsessed, in spite of all the delays and the diversions, I had now reached the focus of the entire enterprise. Against the background of the monotone of the jet flying over the unending sea of clouds, I thought of the sisters who had saved my life—the ones whom I still remembered, and those who, over the years, had become just a dark blue habit with a wide white hat flapping like wings over a featureless face. My sisters.

When I had left I was too young to understand the courage of their protection, too young to thank them properly. Now there were so many things I wanted to know, so many questions I had to ask. But the revolution had come much too late, and the chances of anyone still being alive were slim. And even if they were, after forty-seven years, where would I look for them? Would Jan Urban come up with some useful information? He must, since that was the only hope. I had set aside three days for the personal part of my journey. Three days, perhaps four.

I first met Jan in New York and immediately liked him. Having been at the forefront of the fight against the oppressive regime in his homeland, he now found himself in the midst of the countless challenges of a success story. His boundless energy and natural optimism were contagious. I told him my story and shared with him the dream of searching for the Sisters of Saint Vincent of the small orphanage in Zilina. He promised to help. Tracing them seemed to be an impossible task, and time was running out. And yet some of the sisters could have been in their twenties, which would now put them in their seventies. With luck, they could still be alive.

THE LONG DRIVE toward Bratislava was finally drawing to its end. The outskirts were clearly visible on the horizon, and we pushed hard to get there before darkness. I had been five years old when the family left the house at Gresslingova 52, marking the official end of the "good times." They had turned sour before then, but as long as the family had been able to cling to the external pretense of normalcy, the changes could be kept at some distance. After the war, I took the train from Zilina to Bratislava at least twice, but those had been very short visits, and, being an adolescent, it had never occurred to me to look for our old house. Even now, as we finally entered the city, I was not sure that I would try to go there; after all, I had only a vague idea of its whereabouts, and the street names had been changed several times since. Once again I envied the Swiss; they were part of continental Europe and yet their streets surely retained their names throughout the entire twentieth century. Incredible.

The main artery on which we had made our entrance to the city suddenly ended, and as the intersections appeared I made the turns without any hesitation. The city had grown immensely, and nothing was familiar, and yet the car seemed to drive itself. A few more traffic lights and turns, and we were approaching the bridge across the Danube to Petrzalka. It was the bridge where I had gotten lost as a child—the bridge of my first memory. Suddenly there was a hotel on our right, followed by a small street with a parking space. I switched off the engine and took a deep breath.

"There is something oddly familiar about this place. Our house must be somewhere near."

We started walking and asking passersby about Gresslingova, but nobody seemed to be sure. Even the older people recognized the name only vaguely, indicating that it must be somewhere close by. The walking, however, was also almost automatic, and we quickly navigated the neighborhood, all the time looking for a house with six balconies arranged in two columns. Somehow, the vague

recollection of the balconies that emerged from some archaic folder in my brain's library became the focus, the one
clue to our search. We found ourselves on Red Army Street,
on the odd-numbered side, near number 27. A minute later,
on the opposite side, still at some distance, a house with
balconies was coming into focus. It was the only one that fit
the description, and as our excitement mounted we quickly
counted the intervening houses to anticipate its number.
With some disappointment I realized that it overshot, and
instead of 52 would probably be 56, or even 58. Had I been
following a wrong lead? A mirage from the distant past?

Closing in, just as I was thinking about giving up, I
suddenly realized that three adjacent houses which appeared to be separate—even the shades of their old paint
were different—shared the same number. One needs so
little to be happy. Exhilarated, I realized that the house had
six balconies. But what about "Red Army"? I saw an old
woman slowly walking in front of "my" house, and in the
best tradition of science, using my suddenly available Slovak language, I asked in a neutral tone, "Excuse me, please,
can you tell me where Gresslingova Street is?" She smiled
as if she were about to reveal a secret, and answered, "This
is it. It was Gresslingova in the old times."

And so it happened. I had no wish to enter the apartment where I had spent the first five years of my life, but
the temptation at least to look at the entrance was too great
to resist. We climbed the three floors and for a short while
lingered in front of apartment 16, learning that its present
occupant was an engineer, just like my father. In a sane
world, or even one that was just a little more balanced, I
could have still been living here. But it would have been a
different me, wouldn't it?

•   •   •

JAN URBAN had come through, and we were on our
way to Mendrika, a small village in Bohemia, to meet one
of the sisters from the orphanage. For the first few hours
after leaving Zilina, we drove through beautiful mountains
covered in snow. The roads were icy, and the combination
of the scenery and the ice called for my full attention.
Beyond Olomouc the terrain became flat, and the fog less
demanding. It was then that the events of the last two days
started to drift into my consciousness. As if emerging from
a fog of their own, still unfocused, unsorted, and unedited,
they slowly gained in potency.

First there had been the visit to the nuns at Pezinok,
where one of the sisters was preparing for us detailed
information concerning the Sisters of Saint Vincent from
the orphanage in Zilina. It was there that we heard for the
first time about the hardships during the communist era. It
was odd listening to Sister A., the mother superior, as she
talked about their long ordeal. I had come to reminisce
about mine and instead found myself confronted with
theirs. Sympathy with a mild touch of envy.

The sisters were running a house for elderly priests,
and they proudly showed us the neat little rooms, the
spotless kitchen, and the courtyard where the old and
failing could stroll under the protection of the nuns. Most
impressive, however, was the small grotto for those too
weak to take part in the Holy Mass. There, in the small
enclave overlooking the chapel, they could see the Mass
and, with the help of earphones, listen to it from a safe and
convenient vantage point. Such passive participation in
what constituted the highlight of their daily routine kept

them in touch for a while longer. It was a gentle and thoughtful arrangement, and the nuns were clearly delighted with it.

By the time we left it was almost noon, and the plan to get to Zilina with stopovers in all the meaningful places en route seemed much too ambitious. But we had the information about Sister Koletta, who could be found in the remote village of Mendrika, and nothing else seemed to matter. Suddenly, this long-postponed trip became truly worthwhile.

A childhood collapsed into a brief winter afternoon. Our first stop was Piestany, the initial hiding place after Bratislava. The site of the wonderful summer, the walnuts, the swing in the garden, the bee sting, and the terrifying geese blocking my way home. The glass bridge was still there, and so were the majestic chestnut trees. I did not remember the precise house, but only its general location. It was as if memories were stored in the form of a giant squid, its arms groping in different directions at the same time, sending its brain numerous signals, all partial and imperfect, and yet providing a general, though somewhat amorphous, picture of the surroundings.

Next, the village of Vrbove, now much too big, and our time much too short. The huge synagogue was still there, and so was the church where Judith and I studied catechism. Here the car did not drive itself, and the hectic search for the house where we lived with the Kugels (of baked potatoes fame) was unsuccessful. Were it not for an occasional disappointment, the entire enterprise would have seemed too easy. Half a century was a long time, after all!

We stopped in the town of Trencin, my mother's birthplace. I had forgotten how majestic was the castle that dominated the entire city. It was so close that even a short walk altered its perspective. The two bridges on the Vah near the place where my grandparents lived were intact, and we walked near the river. The trails were frozen, and we walked very slowly. I recalled that my uncle used to take me there to collect beautiful stones. Neither he nor his parents, his sister, or the rest of my mother's family survived Auschwitz. No stones, beautiful or simple, marked their graves. On my mother's grave on the slopes of Mount Carmel was an inscription in memory of her husband. The ultimate reunion.

THIS STRUCK too close to home, and the impact temporarily aborted my reveries. Transposed back to the monotony of driving through the almost flat landscape, I concentrated on the road ahead. The gentle hills were a mixture of forests and open spaces. Sometimes we saw small groups of deer foraging in the fields. Against the background of snow, it was possible to recognize their typical posture even while driving at high speed. It was a pastoral sight, and before long I was back to my musings.

The last segment of the road to Zilina was driven in semidarkness, owing to a combination of fog and air pollution. By the time we reached the city visibility was close to zero, and the road was covered with ice and snow. We made our entry without knowing where we were. It was probably the most fitting way to return: a blind man groping in darkness in his attempt to find the place where he had lost his sight.

Symbolic vanity. At the hotel in Zilina I asked for a suite, as if a room were not sufficient. Coming back to this place, I felt the urge to accentuate the present.

Later in the evening, I could not resist the temptation to take the short walk to the orphanage. The sidewalks were covered with ice, and I was amazed that my feet could still remember how to walk on such a treacherous terrain. There was hardly anyone outside, and the central square was deserted. We entered it from the southeast, just as the lone Russian officer on his white horse had on the day of our liberation. The prominence of the two spires of the chapel and its adjacent orphanage remained untouched. The colonnade around the square was exactly as I had remembered it, and so was the center, with the exception of a tall pine tree, which was new. Everything looked smaller than it was in the mind's landscape, but not that much smaller. Could it be that over the years I had made a partial correction of the memory itself?

Near the heavy door of the orphanage was a plaque indicating that this was now an art gallery. On the wall next to it, in black graffitilike lettering, were two words: "Andy Warhol." An intrusion, almost a violation of privacy.

The medieval street running from the square to our house was much shorter than it ought to have been. Here the memory of the serene events associated with it must have stretched it beyond recognition. I was glad that we had to walk slowly, prolonging the passage to the opening ahead. Although it was January, the traditional Christmas tree was absent. Practically the entire street was absent, its houses razed. Only three remained: the one on the corner;

our own, next to it; and, across the street, the house where the prelate had lived. The church loomed on the right, and the stairs descending to the lower part of the city were intact. At the entrance to our house was a bakery. The entire building was dark. I had no interest in staying any longer, and we made our way back to the hotel in silence.

Places. Places without people. These are the dry bones of memory. The fields of Europe are full of them.

I STARTED TO WORRY about missing the sign to Mendrika. "It is a small road in the fields, barely large enough for a single car," Sister A. had warned. We were past Svitavy, and it should come up any moment now. Obsessively, I stopped the car to inspect all the dirt roads on both sides, although Sister A. had been specific about the turn being on the right.

QUESTION: Why was this meeting so important? Was it just the symbolic act of thanking someone who had been there?

Answer: No. That is probably just a romantic excuse. The real reason—nay, the only reason—is the mystery of Mother Superior. Although she was long dead, I had to learn more about her. What had she been like? Was there anything about her that might explain her outstanding courage? What made her endanger herself, the rest of the nuns, and the entire orphanage in order to save a few Jewish children?

•   •   •

THE SIGN INDICATING Mendrika could be seen
from a distance, and there was no way we could have
missed it. A short drive, and a few scattered houses
emerged from among the snow-covered trees. The church
was surrounded by a building that must have been a castle
in the old times, and we drove into the courtyard. A sister
took us to a small and well-heated guesthouse, promising
to tell Sister Koletta of our arrival. We were expected. A
few minutes later, I saw them approaching.

"Something is wrong. These are not the Sisters of Saint
Vincent." I barely had time to make this disappointing
observation before they entered. In my imagination, the
large white hat had always been a key participant in this
meeting. As I did not know Sister Koletta, the wings above
her head had become the most important thing about her.
But there were no wings, and she looked exactly like the
Benedictine sisters in Pezinok.

And yet, she is genuine. Like myself, she is visibly
excited about the meeting. She is sixty-nine years of age,
having been in her early twenties at the time of my stay in
the orphanage. I don't recall having seen her before, and
neither can she remember me. No, she had not known
then that there were Jews among the children; Mother
Superior had thought it prudent to keep this to herself and
told them only after the war. Yes, she remembers some of
the older boys whom I mention. Fero, who protected me
from abuse in return for my serving as a Hermes between
him and Judith, is a physician in Bratislava. No, she hasn't
been back since 1950, when they were forcibly evicted.
She is glad to learn that the chapel is still exactly as it was.

And when the first opportunity presents itself, she explains why the nuns had to remove the hat in 1964: "'Working in the fields and in the factories, it was impossible to keep the white hat clean and well starched.' I am obviously re- lieved; the unseen hat hovered above her all this time, awaiting recognition.

She tells me about her dream last night. Anticipating our arrival, she sees Sister Anakleta, who used to play the organ in the chapel, and summons her to rise from the dead and come and meet us. Another bridge between us. And thus we spent several hours talking of many things. But mostly we spoke about Mother Superior. The young sister had found her a towering figure, the essence of true devotion and strength of character. These qualities shone even more during the bad times of the communist era. Her exemplary conduct gave the rest of them strength. But my humble verdict is different: she was neither a saint nor a martyr; rather, hers was the power of simple human decency.

We ate at their table, exchanged small gifts, had a photograph of the two of us taken in front of a painting of Saint Vincent, and prepared to leave. As we were parting, I could not resist asking the name of Mother Superior.

"Agatha," she said. "Her name was Agatha."

THE FIELDS OF MEMORY are unbounded. Lo- cations are their servants, and time is their playground. As we travel through life, it is hard to find a truer friend.

A Note About the Author

Shlomo Breznitz was born in Bratislava, Czechoslovakia, in 1936, and received his Ph.D. from the Hebrew University in Jerusalem. He is currently Professor of Psychology at the University of Haifa and at the New School for Social Research in New York, and has published several books on stress and health. He lives with his wife and three children in Israel.

.

A Note on the Type

The text of this book was set in Berkeley Oldstyle, a typeface designed by Tony Stan, based on a face originally developed by Frederick Goudy in 1938 for the University of California Press in Berkeley.

Composed by American–Stratford Graphic Services, Inc.,
Brattleboro, Vermont

Printed and bound by the Haddon Craftsmen, Inc.,
Scranton, Pennsylvania

Designed by Iris Weinstein